A New
Way to WIN

How to Resolve Your Child

Custody Dispute Without Giving Up,

Giving In, or Going Broke

www.ANewWaytoWin.com

Published by the International Center for Peaceful Shared Custody
Book and cover design by Inga Schafer McCuiag
Website design (www.ANewWaytoWin.com) by Inga Schafer McCuaig

This publication is intended to provide accurate information about the subject matters covered. This publication is meant for informational purposes only, and should not be construed as rendering legal, mental health, or other professional services. If expert assistance, legal services, or counseling is needed, the services of a competent professional should be sought.

Names, quotations, and information identifying private individuals have been changed to preserve anonymity. Some examples are alterations of real cases, while other examples are inspired by real cases but are completely fictional.

Printed in the United States of America

First Edition May 2010

ISBN 978-0-578-04935-9
Library of Congress Control Number: 2010901974

"The time for the healing of the wounds has come. The moment to bridge the chasms that divide us has come. The time to build is upon us."

- Nelson Mandela, Inaugural Address, 1994

All proceeds from the sale of this book
are being donated to the non-profit
International Center for Peaceful Shared Custody
in support of its goal of building a global
community of parents helping parents
through separation and divorce.

Acknowledgements

This book would not exist had it not been for the advice, encouragement, and support I received from separated and divorced parents, step-parents and grandparents, family law professionals, colleagues, and my family.

I would like to start by thanking the early endorsers of the book— Bill Eddy, John Hartson, Gay and Kathlyn Hendricks, Lisa Love, Forrest Mosten, Elizabeth Roberts, and Matthew Sullivan. As a first time author, sending my work out for endorsements was both humbling and exciting. Your willingness to review a manuscript from an unknown author speaks volumes about each of you and your authentic commitment to promoting peace.

I want to thank Katie and John Stellar for their help with distilling the core message of this book and with helping to connect the dots. You both have a gift for seeing the intangible links between the creative process on the one hand, and how to communicate it effectively, on the other.

I want to thank Inga Schafer McCuaig for the way she brought the book to life through her cover, book layout and website design. You are a creative genius. I am indebted to Greg Patterson and Carolyn Madison for their help and insights with editing the book and to Phil Whitmarsh for helping me navigate the publishing process.

I would like to express my gratitude to: Charlie Asher, Kay Benton, Mark Desjardins, Michael Desjardins, Jill Forbes, Christer Hokanson, Anne Bingham Newman, Bill Ritchie, Mary Ritchie, Dan Schul, and Mary Sylvester—your comments, ideas, and suggestions helped a great deal.

Finally, I would like to thank my wife Lynn for her unwavering belief in me, and our children Hana, Kai, and Rohan for being their wonderful lovable selves.

Table of Contents

Foreword

Tobias Desjardins is one of the most insightful and dedicated parenting counselors I have ever met. He has wisdom and empathy that has helped many parents over many years—in the U.S. and Canada. I credit him with giving me the light-bulb moment to develop the New Ways for Families program being used in the San Diego family court. With an easy-to-read writing style, Mr. Desjardins makes a convincing case for "winning" a decent parenting arrangement after a divorce. I'm a family law attorney who agrees completely with his strategy.

While I know a few lawyers who just want to generate fees, most of them are misled by the same false belief as their clients that they can "win" something using the old ways. This book truly teaches a *new way* to *win*. Mr. Desjardins' substantial experience shows, in his insights about what really works and what really doesn't work, and in his many practical examples. Parents will save time, anguish, and money by reading this book.

Bill Eddy, LCSW, CFLS
Attorney and Mediator
Author, *High Conflict People in Legal Disputes*
www.HighConflictInstitute.com

Introduction

It only takes one angry parent, step-parent, or grandparent to instigate a destructive custody dispute that eats up thousands of dollars, poisons relationships, and puts children at risk. Once begun, these conflicts take on a life of their own and are fueled by an adversarial family law system that too often brings out the worst in people. So whether you are just breaking up or have been separated for a decade, the information contained here could prove invaluable.

Child custody disputes often come to resemble a no-limit poker game where the kids watch from the sidelines while adults raise the stakes to dangerous levels. Acting under the pretext of doing what's in the best interest of the children, the adults play hand after hand, throwing more and more chips into the already inflated pot. The dispute gets bitter, intractable, and deadlocked.

This is partly because of an alarming trend among some family law attorneys to act as fierce negotiators. Adept at throwing gas on fires, they know all too well that they won't make a dime if their clients find a way to amicably resolve their custody dispute over a coffee at Starbucks. So they push parents to fight for what is "good and just," then disappear when the money runs out.

Interestingly, many custody cases revolve around common issues that families deal with on a regular basis. After a breakup, however, rather than calmly working out differences at the dining room table, they unnecessarily embark upon an emotionally and financially draining process, involving lawyers, depositions, custody evaluators, expert witnesses, and one court date after another.

Imagine a parent in an intact relationship hiring an attorney to work out a parenting problem or write up a household budget. How would someone explain such a thing? "Honey, I know money is tight but a friend at work said that if I asked Mr. Gray here to represent my interests in our budget discussion, I could get those premium cable TV channels we've talked about." It would be absurd. Yet all too often, when a relationship ends, this is exactly the way once rational people start to behave.

Fortunately, there has also been a trend in the other direction. Over the last fifteen years a growing percentage of family law attorneys have embraced the *alternative dispute resolution* (ADR) model. An umbrella term that refers to a group of non-adversarial approaches for resolving conflicts, ADR-focused family law attorneys help parents resolve custody problems in a fair and cost-efficient way outside of the formal court system. Now being taught in law schools around the world, the ADR approach has been shown to be highly effective. Unfortunately, most parents have never heard of it. The "fierce" negotiator types hope they never do.

For the kids, the risks couldn't be higher. Whether they show it or not, children of separation and divorce are deeply affected by their parents' breakup. They love and want a relationship with both parents, no matter how imperfect. However, when a custody battle gets in the way, they can quickly begin experiencing profound levels of anger, fear, and confusion. In very difficult cases, children become so distressed that they may begin to wish they were never born. Some may even have thoughts of suicide.

If you are recently separated or divorced and want to avoid an ugly custody dispute, this book is for you. If you are in a custody battle and have tried everything you can think of to help the kids "win" the game, but have failed, read on. This book will show you the tools that millions of families around the globe are using to resolve their shared custody problems. The concept is simple. You need a new way to win.

The new way to win presented in this book is built on a promise we make to ourselves and our children—a promise to protect all from the serious harm a custody dispute can cause. This is done by:

- Building the children a safe harbor
- Using the "what works" research to develop creative new options
- Having the courage to look within
- Reflecting deeply on what loving our children means, especially in difficult times
- Choosing to be powerful rather than forceful
- Unlocking the power of intention
- Being the most important role model in our children's lives
- Tapping into the wisdom of parents who have walked in our shoes
- Having faith that uncertainty and hardship will lead to insight and healing
- Not being afraid to change course
- Refusing to give up, give in, or go broke.

This is a promise we must commit to in our hearts and make happen with our hands and feet. Protecting children during a breakup is not something we can do by ironing superhero logos on their shirts, getting them on Prozac, or by hiring the super nanny. A "New Way to Win" is leadership. While having the right support in a custody dispute is essential, we must be sure to always lead the way. Our own best interests and the best interests of our kids are at stake. Leadership is especially important if the going gets rough, like when a spouse is unreasonable or chooses to play dirty, as we will see later on.

Whether you are a parent, step-parent, or a grandparent, this book will show you the skills and strategies needed to avoid a custody battle in the first place. If your family is already having custody problems, it will show you how to bring them to an end quickly and peacefully.

Finally, this book is designed to serve as your family's personal lifeboat. Use it to help you through the storm that is your custody situation. Your challenge is to navigate the current and paddle to the other shore—to that place where the dispute is resolved, the kids are thriving, and life is good once again. While the thought of setting out may at first seem intimidating or perhaps even impossible, rest assured that you have everything you need for the journey in these pages.

SECTION ONE:

Laying a Foundation for Change

What Does Winning Mean?

More than anything on that October day in 2004, Sharon wanted her "Judge Judy" moment. She wanted to hear the judge tell her husband Brian how wrong he had been; that all of their trouble could have been avoided had he not walked out on his family, hired a pit bull attorney, and claimed that she was an unfit mother so he could get full custody and avoid paying child support.

She was assured by her attorney that the judge would see through Brian's lies and that truth and justice would prevail. Unfortunately, "Judge Judy" didn't show up in court that day. Five years and seventy thousand dollars later, the custody war continues. All three kids are in counseling, and Sharon drives a twelve-year-old Honda Civic. She can't remember the last time she saw the "Judge Judy" show. Thinking about how much has been lost makes her want to cry.

***

If you had asked Sharon about her expectations at the outset of her ordeal, her answer would not have projected the actual outcome. She is not alone. The parties in custody disputes rarely get what they are seeking and often feel betrayed and battered by the system.

If you were to ask one hundred people what they wanted from a custody dispute, you would likely get as many answers. Some would cite the wellbeing of the kids, others would point to money, property, safety concerns, and so on. The truth is that unlike poker there is no clear definition of what it means to "win" a custody battle. Each situation is unique, its own game, so to speak, requiring its own definition of "winning."

Understanding this helps us to see how and why custody battles spiral out of control. In the example above, Sharon's vision of "winning" was to have the judge scold her ex- husband for his poor choices. As we will see in this section, in custody entanglements only a few ever get want they want. This is because each person in a custody dispute brings to the table their own subjective notion of what "winning" means. A high-conflict dispute involving three children might include twenty or more such notions, those of both parents, the step-parents, the children, each parent's attorney, each child's attorney, the court-based mediator, the child custody evaluator, the court appointed therapists, the parent coordinator, and the judge.

Another complicating factor is that winning a battle doesn't necessarily end the war. This typically happens when parents focus their definition of "winning" more on payback than moving on. Sharon's husband Brian may have left court in 2004 feeling like he had scored a crucial victory, but looking back five years later, he may well regret how he handled things and wish he could do them over. Likewise, Sharon may have really wanted her Judge Judy moment, but how would it have helped? Would it help in your case? While the "winning" issue may seem, on the surface like a complicated and insurmountable problem, there is a rather simple solution.

Imagine that I asked you, and every parent in the world who is in a custody dispute, to put on a special blindfold. This blindfold would cause each person to forget their gender, profession, social and financial status, the identity of their kids, and the reasons why they are fighting for custody. While wearing the blindfold you wouldn't know if you had one kid or ten; whether you lived in Africa or San Diego.[1] Now let's imagine the entire group agreed to participate in a global

---

1   This is a modified version of John Rawls' "Veil of Ignorance" concept as presented in his book *A Theory of Justice*.

conference call where they were challenged to develop an all-purpose definition of what it means to "win" a custody battle. What would the group come up with?

I think they would start by defining "win" in terms of what a judge decides is in the best interests of the kids. The problem with this approach is that ten judges can look at the same case and rule very differently. Under this definition of "win" the parent who has the money for the most persuasive attorney would have a significant advantage over the other parent. Does this sound familiar?

When it came time to cast your ballot, would you vote to adopt this "whoever is strongest" definition? I don't think so. It wouldn't make sense for at least three reasons. The first is that you are blindfolded and you can't remember who you are. You don't know if you are the powerful or the weaker parent, the one with an attorney, or the one on public assistance. The second reason is that this definition has nothing to do with fairness, justice, or integrity.

The final reason has to do with the "win-lose" paradigm. Defining "win" in terms of power and persuasion sets up a situation where one definition of win is pitted against another. It presupposes that the only kind of "win" is the "winner take all" model used in games such as poker or baseball. This is not true. As we shall see in a moment, when sharing custody, a "win-win" model is the ideal.

After rejecting the first definition, I think the group would develop a principle-based definition that sketched out what winning a custody dispute would look like. If one of the blindfolded parents was familiar with the book *Getting to Yes*, he or she might suggest that the group adapt the four key principles found in the book, in the following way:

1. *A win will meet both parties' legitimate shared-custody interests*
   —Unlike in baseball or poker, parents sharing custody need to work with each other after the game is completed, at least until the youngest child is eighteen. If they can't, the situation

19

sinks into one of bitterness and hostility. With shared custody, working for a result that meets everyone's interests, while difficult to do, is essential.

2. *A win will improve your relationship with the kids and your ex-partner* —This may be the one area where the family courts struggle the most. The adversarial court system requires parents to assume a combative posture from day one, further straining already impaired communication and cooperation. While establishing a cordial relationship with a difficult ex may not seem possible—especially if that person has a history of being abusive, is an addict, or has a serious mental health problem—your situation can be improved in a range of ways. One way would be to agree to measures that would end quarrelsome face-to-face contact. Another option would be to work with a shared custody coach or parenting coordinator when a problem arises.

3. *A winning process will be efficient and fair* —Many parents caught up in a custody dispute have told me they sometimes feel like a trapped piece in a lengthy chess game, with little power or influence over the outcome. While the "game" is played out by the lawyers, they, unaware of the rules or their options, are pushed around like mere pawns. Openness, efficiency, and a speedy resolution are crucial to achieving a "win."

4. *A win produces a lasting agreement* —The family court system is good at producing contracts, but not agreements. When a judge makes a ruling, parties are bound by the decision, like it or not. Unfortunately, many of these custody plans break down.

For many families, this means they will be in court for one reason after another, year in and year out, until the youngest child turns eighteen. Mediated agreements, on the other hand, tend to last. Whether arrived at through private mediators or collaborative lawyers, these accords hold up, because the process helps parents to work through the issues in a way that allows everyone, most importantly, the kids, to "win."

Now you may be saying to yourself, "Those ideas sound great—for someone else. You don't know my ex. My ex is not rational." Or perhaps, "My ex is a violent liar. No chance." But you would be wrong. These principles were developed by the authors of *Getting to Yes*, Harvard law professors Roger Fisher and William Ury, to help find winning solutions to some of the world's biggest problems—such as how to win the cold war or bring peace to Northern Ireland, Bosnia, or South Africa.

If this framework can help define what a "win" means for the people of Northern Ireland after decades of extreme violence, it can no doubt help two parents arguing about child support, summer vacation, and which school the kids go to next year.

Understanding The Stakes

Understanding what is at stake in a custody battle is critical. As a child custody mediator and therapist specializing in higher-conflict child custody cases, I've learned that most parents are unaware of how high the stakes are. They fail to realize that how they handle themselves, even if the other parent won't play fair, can mean the difference between their child growing up to be strong and self-reliant, or an angry substance abuser. While this may sound extreme, I assure you it is not.

No parent gets into a custody dispute with the intention of going broke and jeopardizing the welfare of his or her kids. But losing one's life savings and putting children at risk, psychologically if not physically, is often exactly what happens. This is almost always the case when one parent decides not to play fair in order to seek revenge on the other. In this chapter, we will look at the real costs associated with a custody dispute.

THE HUMAN COSTS: HOW DOES SEPARATION OR DIVORCE AFFECT KIDS?

Research into the impact of separation and divorce on kids reveals that most children do fairly well after an initial adjustment period, so long as the following four factors are in place:
- Sound parenting
- An effective shared-custody plan
- Little or no exposure to parental conflict
- Consistent quality time with the non-residential parent

23

When these factors are present, separation or divorce is more likely to promote resilience than emotional or behavioral problems. On the other hand, when these factors are absent, problems are likely to occur. Determining the exact effects a custody battle will have on a child is almost impossible to do. It is a simpler process to determine which kids are more at risk than others.

One of the best predictors that a child will adjust well is whether his or her parents were able to resolve conflicts in a healthy way before their breakup. When absent, parents tend to bring their combative ways with them into the courtroom where the proceedings quickly turn unproductive if not disastrous.

Other risk factors for kids include:
- Violence—history of domestic violence and child abuse
- Drugs—active parental substance abuse
- Change—multiple changes of residence and school
- Friends—absence of peer support
- Money—degree of financial hardship caused by breakup
- New partners—introducing new adult partners to kids too soon after breakup
- Loss of contact—little or no contact with the non-residential parent
- Mental health—debilitating parental mental illness

If a child is struggling with any of the risk factors mentioned, he or she is more likely to struggle with serious long-term problems such as:
- Intense anger—which may be displayed at home, school and in the community
- School problems—including poor grades and problems with teachers and other students
- Substance abuse—more likely to experiment with, and abuse, drugs
- Mental health problems—such as depression and anxiety

- Legal trouble—more likely to get in with the wrong crowd and get into legal trouble
- Teen pregnancy and sexual diseases—more likely to start having sex at a younger age and to engage in unsafe sexual practices
- Running away—most teens who run away are from broken homes
- Risk of suicide—kids may start thinking about suicide when they feel that their situation is unbearable and is unlikely to improve

These are the human stakes connected with fighting over custody. If your children aren't suffering from the nasty side-effects of your dispute, be thankful. But also be careful to look deeply. Seeing the problems our kids are having can be more difficult than it seems. Some children are reluctant to reveal how they really feel. Others may take on the "good child" role, driven subconsciously by the fear of being abandoned. In their minds, if one of their parents can be sent away for not being "good," perhaps the same thing could happen to him or her.

For those of you who see several of the risk factors above in your children, there is good news. While your kids might currently be on the wrong path, there is a great deal you can do to turn things around, even if your ex won't play fair. Ways to do just that will be presented in each of the following chapters in this book.

THE FINANCIAL COSTS

In a memorable scene in the movie Jerry Maguire, sports agent Maguire (Tom Cruise) says to his client Rod Tidwell (Cuba Gooding Jr.) over the phone, "Tell me what I can do for you?" Tidwell, in a low voice that slowly builds, says "It is a very personal and very important thing. Are you ready, Jerry? Show me the money. Say it with me,

Jerry—with meaning. I need to feel you baby. *SHOW ME THE MONEY.*"

A step-parent once told me that he felt as if everyone he dealt with in his new wife's custody battle was saying, "Show me the money." I can understand why. Over five years, they had spent more than $250,000 on legal fees, two custody evaluations, the child's attorney, three therapists, and a visitation monitor. While this is an extreme example, the average contested divorce in the United States costs each parent between $20,000 and $30,000. No one begins their custody dispute saying, "I have 30,000 bucks in the bank and I'm going to blow it all on this thing." Little by little, however, the expenses mount, until suddenly, the bank account is empty.

What if there was a way to predict how much more money you are likely to spend on your custody dispute, the value of the chips you have yet to put into the pot? Perhaps you are already in a case and want to know how much it will cost if things keep going as they are. There is a way to make these calculations.

Step One: *How often will you go to court?*
How often is the average higher-conflict custody dispute back in court?

a. Every 6 months   b. once a year   c. every 2 years

d. Every 5 years

The answer is b.[2]

---

[2]   I wish I could point you to a stack of research studies to back this claim up. Unfortunately, the little scholarly work that is available on the subject of how often higher conflict custody cases return to court does not lend itself well to the kind of broad generalization I am making. This is in large part because the variables in each custody dispute are different. So you might say that, after talking with many family law professionals about this issue, the answer (once/year) is my best "guess" on the subject.

Step Two: *How much have you spent over the last twelve months?*
Think about how much money you have spent on your custody battle
over the last twelve months (on lawyers, evaluations, therapists, etc).
Then add to that the amount of money you didn't earn as a result of
missing work (for court or because of sickness, etc.) and the value of
the business opportunities you lost or couldn't capitalize on, because
you were tied up fighting over custody.
$_____

Step Three: *How long until the youngest child turns eighteen?*
How many years will it be until the youngest child in your custody
dispute turns eighteen?

_____

Step Four: *Add it all up*
Assuming you will be back in court once a year (the average), take the
amount you came up with in step two and multiply it by the number
you came up with in step three. For example, let's say you have spent
$3000 in the last year on your custody dispute, and your youngest is
eight years old. You would multiply $3000 X 10 and your total would
be $30,000.

_____($ you spent over the last year) x _____ (# of years until
youngest child turns eighteen) = _____

This is the money you haven't spent yet. Think of it as poker chips
sitting in front of you that you can still choose to walk away with. You
may be thinking, "Where would I get that kind of cash for my custody
case?" Like most, you would max out your credit, pass on the vacation
you had planned, cash in your savings bonds, get a second job, take
out a second mortgage, or borrow from grandma.

Each step of the way a little voice inside of you will be screaming "No, no more. Enough." Then that other voice will counter, "I've come this far. I can't walk away now. I'm in too deep." On and on it will go. And all the while your children are suffering, because you can't afford to buy them the things they want or need.

Assuming that you will spend $30,000 on your custody dispute, here are some other things you might have used that money for:

- 600 passes to Disneyland
- 1000 lunches at Chucky Cheese
- 2000 pepperoni pizzas
- 14,500 ice creams at Baskin Robins
- 750 tickets to see a major-league baseball game or the ballet
- A piano and 580 private lessons
- A horse and riding lessons for fifteen years
- 1500 trips for two to the movies
- One-week cruise every year for you and your kids
- A college degree
- Invested at ten percent, you would have $60,000 in seven years—and $120,000 in fourteen years

The purpose of this chapter was to help you cut through the misinformation about the costs involved in child custody disputes. Fighting over custody can not only be financially devastating, it can literally mean the difference between your kids growing up happy and healthy or developing serious problems with regards to relationships, mental health, and general coping skills.

Are You Dealing with a High-Conflict Person?

Eighty percent of family court cases are referred to as low-conflict cases. These are the ones where the parents process their separation or divorce amicably and at relatively low cost, both financially and in terms of harm to children. The remaining twenty percent of cases are considered the conflict cases. This group can be broken down further into moderate-conflict and high-conflict, with each representing about ten percent of the overall number of cases.

Over the last decade a great deal of research has focused on child custody issues and the factors that determine conflict level. Let's now look at some of the findings.

WHAT DOES A HIGH-CONFLICT CUSTODY DISPUTE LOOK LIKE?

In his article, *The Early Identification and Streaming of Cases of High-Conflict Separation and Divorce* (2001), Dr. Ron Stewart explains that high-conflict custody disputes can be identified by the presence of a distinct set of markers. The more markers present, the more likely it is that the case involves high-conflict:

- One or both parents have a history of criminal convictions
- A child protection agency is involved in the dispute
- One or both parents have made several lawyer changes
- The case is continually in and out of court
- The court case drags on for months or years

- There is a history of the court denying one or both parents access to the child or requiring that their access be supervised by a visitation monitor
- One or both parents have a history of mental health problems including, but not limited to, depression, anger, withdrawal and non-communicative behavior
- History of violent and abusive behavior while the parental relationship was intact
- A tendency to vilify anyone perceived to be aligned with the other parent
- Inability to see the difference between their needs and the child's needs
- Rigid and inflexible thinking about relationships and child development
- High degree of distrust and a history of poor boundaries
- A tendency to involve the children in the custody dispute
- A pattern of aligning with the child or alienating the child from the other parent

WHAT FUELS THE CONFLICT?

In one of the finest books ever written on the dynamics of separation and divorce conflict, *In the Name of the Child*, the writers explain that parents in higher-conflict child custody cases are stuck at a critical impasse in which they can see no way out but to keep fighting.

These impasses, according to authors Janet Johnston, Vivienne Roseby, and Kathryn Kuehnle, are fueled by multiple factors including: the adversarial nature of the court system; pit-bull attorneys; negative cheerleaders such as family and friends who encourage fighting; mental health or other professionals who become aligned with one side; fear because of a history of domestic violence while the relationship was intact and since; denial or ambivalence about the relationship being over; the lingering effect of a traumatic separation;

and intense vulnerability to powerful feelings such as abandonment, shame, fear, and loss.

RAYMOND'S STORY

Raymond was thirteen, and his brother Adam was eleven when they walked into my counseling office with their dad for the first time. Raymond's mom and dad had been together for fifteen years when they filed for divorce. During that time, both parents had good jobs, owned a home, two cars, and a dog. While their relationship had been troubled, it would have been impossible to predict that, seven years after getting divorced they would be seeking help—because their oldest son wanted to kill himself.

During a two-hour visit in my office, I came to learn that the parents of Raymond and Adam had been engaged in a ferocious custody battle. So bad was the fighting, that the family law courts routinely referred the case to child protective services. This resulted in the kids being placed in foster care twice, for a year each time. All of the material goods the parents had once owned were now gone. Neither had a job, health insurance, or a family law attorney. For the last two years they had represented themselves in a battle that had long since lost its direction and meaning. The parents seemed to be fighting merely for the sake of not giving up.

After dealing with the initial crisis, I thought carefully about whether this case was too high-conflict for me. Looking back, I can now see that I was in over my head. These parents were not looking for someone to help their son; they wanted me to see only their side of the dispute and to join in their crusade against the other.

Despite my concerns, I did agree to see Raymond in counseling. I tried to help him work through some of the anger he had for his parents. While I tried, I wasn't able to help this family as much as I would have liked. Still, I am glad I got involved with the case because

31

something happened that would forever change my understanding of how custody disputes affect kids.

Late one afternoon, the two boys and their dad arrived at my office, without an appointment, asking if I could meet with them briefly to work through a problem. None of us knew it, but this would be our last session. The truth was that counseling had not been going well. This had a lot to do with the fact that Raymond and his brother mostly refused to talk to me. I couldn't blame them. The boys had learned over the years that what they said to therapists had a way of coming back to haunt them. Their parents had a bad habit of taking what their children said in counseling and using that information to launch a new attack on the other parent in court.

When Raymond refused to answer a question I had put to him, his father became frustrated and threatened to ground him if he didn't cooperate. Suddenly animated, Raymond stood up to his father, literally, getting out of his chair and glaring at the intimidating 6' 5", 250-pound man. The father turned red with anger and met his son's stare. The tension was palpable; it was clear that this was the first time the thirteen-year-old had dared to stand up to his dad.

As I tried to defuse the situation with gentle urging, what happened next caught me completely off guard. Raymond calmly walked over to his father and stood in front of him. Dad, clearly feeling provoked, stood and turned to face his son. They were toe to toe, looking squarely at each other. Neither said a word. Several seconds passed. Then Raymond spat in his dad's face.

For about ten seconds, no one in the room moved. It was as if, suddenly, the tension in the room had frozen us all in place. Dad moved first, turning to me for my reaction. I remember vividly the intense anger in his eyes. Behind that, it seemed, he realized this was not simply a random act of disrespect by a thirteen-year-old. It was a statement—one that Raymond had delivered hundreds of times to his parents, in just as many ways.

Early in the custody battle, his requests were delivered on Hallmark cards. Seven years later, when I met them for the first time, the request was part of his suicide note. On the day of our last counseling session, it was delivered through the act of spitting in his dad's face. The message was always the same, "Please stop all the fighting. Please. Please. I want to love you both." Unfortunately, these words always fell on deaf ears.

***

Looking back, I think Dad was trying to listen, but something kept the message from sinking in. As you will see shortly, the inability to hear those around you, to look within and reflect on constructive criticism, are some of the defining features of a higher-conflict personality.

Interestingly, I met Dad again two years later when he was ordered by the Family Law court to complete a high-conflict co-parenting education program that I offer in Southern California. In that time he had remarried, had a daughter, and was now in a high-conflict custody battle with his new ex.

According to Bill Eddy, a family law attorney, psychotherapist, and the author of *High Conflict People in Legal Disputes*, certain people have what he calls a high-conflict personality (HCP), making it more likely that any contest they enter will turn ugly. Through the High-Conflict Institute, Mr. Eddy teaches family court judges, attorneys, mental health professionals, and parents, strategies for working more effectively with HCP.

Higher-conflict people tend to have some or many of the following traits:

- Crave the limelight—need to be the center of attention

33

- Seem to enjoy conflict—they see it as a core and normal element in relationships
- Want it all their way—tend to think in black and white terms, as in, " it's my way or the highway."
- Struggle in relationships—a history of serious problems getting and staying in healthy relationships
- Can be vengeful—will seek out to punish
- Will be dishonest when it suits them—have little trouble lying or being deceitful
- Seek to control others—tend to manipulate, dominate and control others
- Prefer throwing gas rather than water—will choose to escalate a conflict rather than compromise
- Are not trusting—can be jealous, paranoid and mistrustful
- Like to blame others—prefer to blame others rather than take responsibility, even for small things
- See themselves as a victim—will cast themselves as a victim when it benefits them
- Aggressive—can be very violent
- Tend to avoid feelings of grief and loss—have a hard time grieving
- Attachment problems—struggle with feelings of being left behind or abandoned
- Poor insight—lack the ability to look within
- Highly emotional—tend to allow their emotions to rule their lives
- Fiercely competitive—the prospect of losing is so threatening that they will do whatever it takes to win
- Hold grudges—have difficulty forgiving
- Poor boundaries—tend to blur boundaries in adult relationships and as a parent
- Chronically feel empty inside—struggle with persistent feelings of emptiness
- Lack empathy—are often blind to the impact their behavior has on the people around them

- Self sabotage—they tend to undermine themselves
- Don't want help—resist or flat out believe they don't need it

The defining feature of this group is a combination of three traits: a lack of insight into their own strengths and weaknesses, a very high level of defensiveness, and a lack of empathy for how their behavior negatively impacts those around them. You might think of this combination as being almost like a vest that is so tight-fitting it prevents the person from growing emotionally the way the rest of us do by looking within, reflecting on criticism, and paying attention to how our actions affect others.

This doesn't mean higher conflict-people are easy to identify in a crowd. The opposite is true. That is partly because all of us have a high-conflict trait or two. It is also because high-conflict people are doctors, carpet layers, lawyers, grocery clerks, taxi drivers, fire fighters, veterinarians, computer programmers, and postal clerks. In fact, one of the truly confusing things about high-conflict people is that one day they can be charismatic, charming, and exciting to be around, and the next they can be hostile, belligerent, and aggressive.

The most important thing to know about these folks is that they do custody disputes differently. They play by a different set of rules—a set of rules that can be very confusing for their opponent to make sense of. This is because their behavior in a dispute is not so much directed at resolving the problem, but rather at soothing their own, often overwhelming, level of internal distress.

Part of the way they do this is by telling themselves a story, inside of their own heads, about what is going on. Higher conflict people will say the following things to themselves—despite the fact that there is little or no justification for feeling this way:

- My needs are more important than anyone else's—especially my ex's
- My child will benefit no matter how tough the fight

35

- I know what is best for my child—my ex has no clue
- I may need to retaliate if things don't go my way
- My ex is an unfit parent—I should have one-hundred percent custody
- My child would be better off never seeing the other parent again
- I have to win this battle no matter what the cost
- Once the court hears my side, I will win

WHAT ARE THE LEVELS OF CUSTODY CONFLICT?

In their book *Caught in the Middle: Protecting the Children of High-Conflict Divorce* (1994), Carla Garrity and Mitchell Baris sketch out the following five levels of conflict:

Level One – Parents are able to communicate with each other in a way that is validating, empowering, and respectful. Both parents are able to separate their own needs from those of the children and are generally effective at resolving conflicts without exposing the children to overt expressions of anger or other negative emotions. Raising the children is done in a spirit of cooperation.

Level Two – Shared custody conflicts between the parents will at times involve verbal quarrelling in front of the children. One or both parents may question the child about the other parent's personal life, talk disparagingly about the other parent to the child, or even try occasionally to form an alliance with the child against the other parent.

Level Three – Shared custody conflicts will involve loud arguments most commonly on the phone or at a pick-up or drop-off location. Typically the parents will have a history of being verbally abusive with each other, but their conflicts don't involve threats or a history of physical violence. One or both parents will talk badly about the other parent to the child, will threaten to go back to court to limit the other parent's access to the child, and will make repeated attempts to engage the child in a coalition against the other parent around isolated and often trivial issues. One or both parents may struggle with substance use or abuse issues.

Level Four – Child custody conflicts escalate to the point where they emotionally harm the child. Interactions between the parents may involve such things as slamming doors, throwing things, stalking, and possibly even threats of kidnapping. Police and child protection involvement is not uncommon. One or both parents may try to directly involve the child in the dispute by attempting to firmly align the child against the other parent. The parents will be in court on an ongoing basis. One or both parents may have engaged a highly-aggressive attorney. One or both parents may struggle with substance abuse and/or a mild to moderately impairing mental illness.

Level Five –In addition to the presence of the factors associated with level four, there is a history of physical, sexual, or severe emotional abuse. One or both parents have a serious addiction issue and or/a severely impairing mental illness.

In conclusion, I urge you to assess the level of conflict in your dispute. But don't focus only on your former spouse. Make sure you also look at yourself, the step-parents, the attorneys, and anyone else who is playing a key role in your situation. If you believe that you are dealing with moderate to high-conflict, please remember that knowledge is power. If your situation involves such issues as: alienation, sexual abuse, parental alienation, visitation resistance, higher-conflict personalities, stalking, or child abuse, it is essential that you read what the experts in these areas have to say.

I also strongly recommend that you read on. The upcoming chapters will introduce you to a spectrum of skills, strategies, and options for turning things around.

Options They Don't Want You to Know About

It may surprise you to learn that over the last twenty years several very affordable alternatives to fighting in family court have been proven in university studies to be highly effective. What's more, thousands of professionals (mostly lawyers and mental health professionals), have completed training in these approaches at law schools in the United States and around the world. These approaches are so widely known, that every family law attorney on the planet knows about them. Regrettably, too many of them are keeping it a secret.

Why is this? The answer is simple—you guessed it—money. You have it and they want it. Let's face it, if at the end of your initial consult with a family law attorney that person said, "By the way the lawyer down the hall will help you work out your mess at one-tenth the cost and in a fraction of the time," you would start walking. At least I hope you would. For two decades you have had the option of doing just that. Unfortunately, most parents are unaware that such an option even exists.

Collectively these approaches are referred to as your Alternative Dispute Resolution (ADR) options (the term External Dispute Resolution is used in some countries). Essentially, ADR refers to a collection of approaches that are designed to resolve disputes without the headaches and expense of going to court. So effective are these approaches at reducing the costs involved in resolving conflicts, that they are being widely used in areas including business, government, and healthcare.

In the family law area, ADR approaches are increasingly popular. This is because they: give parents control over the selection of the people who will help resolve their dispute, are typically confidential, are conducted in a timely manner, tend to produce lasting agreements and cost much less than fighting in court.

The ADR approaches you may want to consider using in your situation can be divided into three areas:
1. Learn
2. Resolve
3. Move on

LEARN

Had you and your ex stayed together, parenting your kids would have been challenging. It is for all of us. Now that you are separated or divorced, it's going to be even more so. One reason why parents frequently return to family court has to do with the fact that they never developed an effective shared-custody plan in the first place. Instead of reading a book like this or attending a brief class, they make the crucial mistake of going blindly into the negotiation process, or worse—trusting an unscrupulous attorney to "work things out."

Usually referred to as co-parenting or divorce education classes, these programs teach parents how to share custody well. Mandatory in many places, the topics usually include: the impact of custody conflict on kids, levels of conflict, types of shared custody plans, stress management, problem solving, mediation, and court preparation.

For parents wanting to access co-parenting education training online, there are a range of choices. Barb and Charlie Asher, through the Freedom 22 Foundation, have developed three outstanding programs: www.UpToParents.org is for divorcing parents, www.ProudToParent.org is for parents who were never married and are now separating, and www.WhileWeHeal.org is for parents who are considering separation or divorce but want to try and work through their problems. All three programs are available at no charge.

The Center for Divorce Education, an Ohio-based non-profit, offers the widely acclaimed *Children in the Middle* program. Developed by Dr. Don Gordon, Ph. D., and Jack Arbuthnot, Ph.D., the program has been endorsed by judges, lawyers, mediators, psychologists, and teachers, all over the world. Recognized as a "model program" by the Substance Abuse and Mental Health Services Administration (SAMHSA), *Children in the Middle* offers an evidence-based curriculum that has been shown in university studies to be very effective. The program is available in English and Spanish at www. Divorce-Education.com. A program for parents in high-conflict disputes, called *After the Storm*, is also available through the Center for Divorce Education, though not online.

For parents who would rather read a book than attend an in-person or online program, several excellent resources are available including: *Mom's House Dad's House: Making Two Homes for Your Child*, by Isolina Ricci, and *Planning for Shared Parenting: A Guide for Parents Living Apart*, published by the Massachusetts Chapter of the Association of Family and Conciliation Courts (AFCC).

One of the most important things that people learn in the Getting Prepared stage is that there are two types of shared custody plans, one for low-conflict and one for moderate to high-conflict. This distinction is important, because the plan given out by most court-based mediators, usually referred to as a *Cooperative Plan*, is designed for lower-conflict situations. Cooperative shared-custody plans work well when both parents are able and willing to work together in a spirit of good faith.

The problem is that cooperative plans don't work in moderate to high-conflict situations, and tend to make things worse. When a situation involves a history of violence, child abuse, serious addictions, bitter conflict, revenge, or not being able to make decisions jointly, a cooperative plan is not recommended.

The type of plan that is needed in a moderate- to high-conflict situation is referred to as a *Parallel Plan*. Such plans emphasize: minimal contact between parents, often only via e-mail so all communications are documented; transitioning to a business-like relationship where only essential parenting issues are discussed; and the importance of having a detailed and written plan. You can think of a parallel plan as imposing a structure that resembles two railroad tracks running side by side. The tracks lead in the same direction, but both parents are expected to drive their own train.

Parallel plans are shaped to fit the unique needs of each situation. For example, in a case where there is a history of violence or one parent wants to re-establish a relationship with a child after a long absence, a parallel plan could include supervised visitation provisions. It might also include a "step-down" protocol that would allow the violent or absent parent increasing levels of access to the child, but only after meeting specific criterion set out in the court-approved plan.

I'm sure you can see why it is important to get prepared before diving into the task of negotiating a custody plan. It is essential that parents figure out the answers to several key questions, including:

- What does "win" mean?
- What are the stakes?
- What level of conflict am I dealing with?
- What kind of a shared custody plan do I need?

One additional resource you may want to consider using is the www. OurFamilyWizard.com suite of co-parenting tools. This site offers parents an easy way to manage just about every aspect of their co-parenting relationship online. An excellent tool for reducing conflict, *Our Family Wizard* helps parents communicate better and more effectively coordinate their schedules, expenses, and other co-parenting responsibilities.

RESOLVE

Once you are prepared, it's time to go to the next phase—resolving your dispute. ADR offers parents three main options: *do-it-yourself, collaborative divorce, and private mediation*. It doesn't matter whether a family is just getting divorced or has been fighting over custody for years; these approaches are specifically designed to help them work things out.

Resolving Your Dispute: Option One—Do It Yourself

More and more parents are using ADR principles to resolve their custody disputes on their own. In lower-conflict situations this might be done over a coffee at Starbucks. In moderate- to high-conflict situations, the process might involve a series of e-mails. If this option appeals to you, there are several things you should consider:

Make sure you are ready. Before trying to resolve your dispute on your own, it is essential that you do your homework. Don't reach out impulsively after reading this section and invite your ex to meet you for dinner to "work things out." Before moving forward with this idea, I strongly recommend that you finish reading this book.

Use the "what works" research. It is important that you think through in detail how you would like your custody plan to look. Use the research literature on how to build a strong custody plan to help you visualize a plan that will work for your family. Make sure to incorporate ideas into your plan that your ex will support.

Get the legal help you need. Getting good legal advice is very important when developing a solid custody plan. This leads some parents to resist the do-it-yourself approach, because they are intimidated by the legal aspects associated with developing a custody plan on their own. Fortunately, there are several ways that parents can access the legal assistance they need without having to max out their credit cards.

43

One way to do this is to work with a lawyer who offers "unbundled legal services." While not available everywhere, this option allows parents to pay for only those legal services they want (e.g. advice, document review, coaching on how to present an issue in court, etc.) and do the rest themselves. Unbundled services are paid for by the hour, and don't usually involve the payment of a retainer.

Some parents choose to each hire their own "unbundled" attorney. In such cases, the lawyer might be thought of as a consultant whose job it is to advise their client on the family law issues relevant to their case. When it comes to working things out, however, these lawyers stay in the background. It is up to the parents, not the attorneys, to resolve their dispute.

Parents with low incomes can access similar assistance, usually at little or no cost, through legal aid clinics. Often offered through local Bar Associations or community-based non-profit groups, these programs connect parents with low incomes to family law attorneys who can help them.

If you are planning to use a do-it-yourself approach, I strongly encourage you to meet with an unbundled or a legal aid lawyer before you take any legal action in your separation or divorce. You will get a much better idea of your rights and responsibilities, as well as good and bad strategies. It will also help you avoid some possibly serious mistakes that self-representing people can make.

With regard to completing and submitting forms to the family court, most jurisdictions provide parents with online access to the forms they need. Parents who require help completing the forms can usually meet with a facilitator at the courthouse—without an appointment. As an alterative to working with a court facilitator (the lines can be long), you may want to consider hiring a paralegal professional. Specialists in the preparation of legal documents, a good paralegal will help ensure that your forms and documents are prepared and submitted to the court properly.

Propose the do-it-yourself option carefully. The way you present this idea to your ex is going to be very important. I suggest that you write your ex a letter that briefly, and in a friendly way, sketches out the advantages and disadvantages of trying to work things out on your own.

Don't try and write or talk like lawyer. As you go through the do-it-yourself process try to avoid using legal jargon or writing your proposals or agreements using complicated sentences. Keep things as simple as possible. Nolo Press publishes an excellent do-it-yourself resource for parents wanting to draft their own custody plan. *Building a Parenting Agreement That Works: How to Put Your Kids First When Your Marriage Doesn't Last*, by Mimi Lyster, offers detailed advice on how to build an effective custody plan. The book also includes downloadable forms that can be used to write your plan.

Don't give up. This approach doesn't always work. Sometimes parents are able to work several issues out, but get stuck on one or two. Sometimes they get nowhere. Whatever happens in your case, don't give up on finding a peaceful way to resolve your dispute. You may be closer than you realize to working things out. Instead of throwing in the towel, I suggest that you consider working with a private child custody mediator or a collaborative divorce professional.

RESOLVING YOUR DISPUTE: OPTION TWO—PRIVATE CHILD CUSTODY MEDIATION

Private mediation and court-based mediation are very different, and it is important that you understand how and why.

Court-based mediation is typically a mandatory process where both parents are ordered to appear at the court house and meet with a mediator. In the time allotted, the mediator's job is to help both parents work out an agreement. If an agreement is not reached, many jurisdictions require that the mediator then make written recommendations to the judge suggesting possible solution options. In deciding the case, the judge may or may not agree to order the mediator's recommendations.

Court-based mediation can be an effective resource for parents in a lower-conflict custody dispute that can be worked out in one hour or less. For parents in a moderate- to high-conflict dispute, court-based mediation is typically ineffective, and in some cases makes things worse. There are five reasons for this.

Lets play beat the clock. The length of time allotted for the court-based mediation process is usually one hour. In a typical moderate- to high-conflict case, both parents have between five and eight issues that they feel need to be resolved. Trying to do this in a one-hour session means that each parent will have approximately five minutes to present each of their concerns and negotiate a resolution. It's not realistic.

No one said I had to come prepared. Too few parents prepare for their court-based mediation session. They don't take the time to learn the basics about negotiating or how to share custody effectively. Instead they go into the process nervous, blind, and tired because they couldn't sleep the night before. As a result things go poorly, and little if anything is actually accomplished.

One size fits all. Given the overwhelming number of cases that court-based mediators see and the volume of shared-custody plans that they help build, they tend to use the same basic template with everyone. I often ask the question in my workshops, "If I had each of you tape to the wall the custody plan your court-based mediator gave you—one next to the other—and then each of you walked by and looked at them, what would you notice?" The answer of course is that they all look practically identical. Each parent's situation is unique—but everyone has the same plan.

Watch what you say. In many jurisdictions, when a mediation session doesn't produce an agreement, the mediator stops acting as a neutral helper and becomes an evaluator who makes written recommendations to the judge. This is an important dynamic, because it changes the process from one where the parents can be open and honest with each other to one in which they need to be careful what they say so as not to be seen in a negative light by the "soon-to-be" evaluator.

The possibility of the mediator turning into an evaluator can change the process into something resembling a public-relations exercise, where the parties are more focused on winning favor with the mediator than on actually working things out. Changing hats from mediator to evaluator is also problematic, because of the time issue. Is one hour really enough time for the mediator-turned-evaluator to make sense of the many variables in a custody dispute and thoughtfully make recommendations that will genuinely help improve things? Of course it isn't.

Don't agree to anything. It is not uncommon for parents to tell me that their lawyer instructed them not to agree to anything in court-based mediation. Instead, they are encouraged to stay focused on winning. Obviously, this tactic completely undermines the mediation process.

For the five reasons listed above, many parents conclude that mediation won't work in their situation. Who can blame them? They're right. Well, sort of. What they should be saying is court-based mediation won't work. There is a big difference between court-based mediation and private mediation. The problem is that most parents don't know that private mediation even exists.

Private child-custody mediation, on the other hand, is a purely voluntary process where a neutral third party (usually an attorney

47

or a mental health professional) assists the parents in reaching a fair agreement. The parents make the decisions, not the mediator. During the process, the focus is on helping both parents create a lasting agreement that meets their needs, goals, and interests. When a final agreement is reached, it is filed with the family law court and becomes a court order. If the process proves unsuccessful, and a final agreement is not reached, the parties can choose to work with a collaborative team (see below) or go to court.

Private mediation has several distinct advantages over court-based mediation:

It's confidential. In the 1960s' television show *Get Smart*, Agent 86 (Maxwell Smart) would use a "dome of silence" when discussing top secret information. Private mediation is a little bit like negotiating under the *Get Smart* "dome of silence." At the beginning of the private mediation process both parents sign a confidentiality agreement making it clear that: nothing said during the mediation sessions can be admitted into court, that the mediator cannot be called to testify on behalf of either parent, and that the mediator will not make recommendations to the court.

Under the "dome of silence" parents are free to speak openly and directly with each other without worrying that one will use what is said against the other in court. Or that, once his or her shoe-phone starts ringing, the mediator will turn into an evaluator and start making all kinds of recommendations to the court.

Parents are in control. One big advantage of private mediation is that parents remain in full control. Only parents decide on the issues that are important to them. Then with the help of the neutral mediator, they negotiate an agreement. No one makes decisions for them.

The process is quick. Private mediation is more time-efficient than a drawn-out court battle. On average, parents participate in three to six sessions, each lasting between one and two hours.

Create a plan that fits and lasts. The emphasis in private mediation is on producing a plan that uniquely fits the needs of the children and both parents. By doing this there is a much greater chance that the agreement will last.

Your legal rights are protected. It is recommended that each of the parents review the final agreements with their own attorneys before signing them, so as to ensure that their rights are being protected by law.

It can be used anytime to solve implementation problems. Private mediation can be used at the start of a separation or divorce to hash out an agreement on finances, property, and child custody issues. It can also be used at any point thereafter to work out a custody issue before it blows up into something that has parents wanting to return to court. In such cases, once the new issue is resolved an amendment to the overall custody plan is filed with the court.

It is much less stressful than going to court. In private mediation, instead of presenting your case to a judge, your job is to explain your concerns to your ex and use the neutral mediator to help you work out solutions. This makes things much less stressful and far more productive.

Saves you thousands of dollars. Compared to the heavy financial outlay of a court battle, the cost of private mediation is a drop in the bucket. Usually parents share the mediator's fee equally and then pay for the consult with their own attorney. Depending on how complicated the mediation process turns out to be, each parent could spend 95 percent less on private mediation than what they would have spent fighting in court.

49

Finally, private mediation is not appropriate in all situations. In some cases, because of a history of violence within the relationship, a parent won't feel comfortable in the same room with his or her ex and might even be afraid of reprisals or physical harm. Even in such cases, accommodations can be made that allow parents to try the mediation process. For example, parents might attend the sessions individually or participate by telephone or video conference.

RESOLVING YOUR DISPUTE: OPTION THREE— COLLABORATIVE DIVORCE

According to the International Academy of Collaborative Professionals, Collaborative Divorce is a new way for parents to resolve disputes respectfully—without going to court—while working with trained professionals. The heart of Collaborative Divorce (also called "no-court divorce," "divorce with dignity," and "peaceful divorce") is to offer parents the support, protection, and guidance of working with their own lawyers without having to go to court.

In terms of process, collaborative divorce involves a series of in-person meetings with your ex where both attorneys attend. In some cases, depending on the issues involved, collaboratively-trained experts, such as mental health or financial professionals, will also attend. The focus of the meetings is to identify each parent's interests, needs, priorities and goals and to help them develop a fair settlement.

While this process may sound like court without a court room or a judge, it isn't. Forrest Mosten, one of the pioneers in this field eloquently explains in his new book, *Collaborative Divorce Handbook: Helping Families without Going to Court* (2009), that the difference is attitude. Mosten explains that as a young family law attorney, "I was told that a good settlement is when everyone feels badly, because all of the parties feel as if they lost. The collaborative definition of a good settlement is that everyone feels good, because all parties feel that they got as many of their needs met as possible."

Far less costly than a drawn-out court battle, the Collaborative Divorce process helps parents craft a fair settlement in a way that reduces anxiety and fear. The end result is a tailor-made agreement that is much more likely to reflect the unique needs of the parties, than an order issued by an overworked judge.

Finally, even if you don't think the collaborative process will work in your situation (e.g. the other parent wants to fight in court), I strongly encourage you to consider working with an attorney who has Collaborative Divorce training and experience. Experts at peacefully resolving custody disputes, both in the courtroom and outside of it, collaboratively trained lawyers are strong team players who will guide your situation in the right direction.

MOVE ON

Once the negotiations are over, whether you've come away with a contract or an agreement, the next step is to make it work in the real world. Similar to a marriage, a shared-custody plan is easier to get into than to make work. As you have already learned, there is much riding on how well you put the terms of your negotiated deal into practice.

Over the last decade two ADR options have emerged to help parents "make it work." Given how recently they've appeared, it's likely that neither you nor your friends and family have heard of either Shared Custody Coaching or Parent Coordination.

Making It Work: Option One—Shared-Custody Coaching

A shared-custody coach (often referred to as a co-parenting coach or a divorce coach) is a neutral professional who helps divorced or separated parents implement their custody plan. Typically offered by a mental health worker with specialized training, shared custody coaching helps parents work out problems before little issues turn into big (and costly) ones.

A voluntary program that parents pay for themselves, the advantages of coaching include:

- Expert advice as required: Coaches are available when needed and only bill if and when parents use their services.
- Continuity: You don't have to explain your situation over and over again to someone new every time you want a little advice.
- One or both parents: While it's ideal to have a coach work with both parents, given that this is a voluntary program not all parents want a coach's services. As a result, it's common to find a coach working with just one parent, helping that person better manage their side of things.
- Convenience: Coaching work is typically done by phone, conference call, video conference, or e-mail.
- High-conflict accommodation: Because coaching is done by phone or via the internet, it can be an effective resource for a parent dealing with a high-conflict ex.
- Documentation for court: Should a situation arise where the parents return to court, the coach can provide a written statement as to the efforts made by the parent (or both parents) to work things out.
- Great value: Coaches tend to charge a fraction of what an hour with a lawyer costs. If working with a coach saves just one trip back to court with an expensive attorney in tow, it will have been worth it.
- Peace of mind: Many parents find it comforting to know that there is a familiar person—and a person familiar with their situation—to turn to when help is needed.

Finally, parents all over the world are dealing with the same shared-custody headaches. Dealing with an uncooperative ex is difficult whether you live in London, Sydney, Ottawa, Los Angeles, or Cape

Town. Fortunately, the tools used by coaches to help parents improve their situations are built on universal principles that apply, regardless of nationality, race, gender, ability, or sexual-orientation. Once this is understood, it becomes clear that parents have a global community of coaches from which to choose.

Making It Work: Option Two—Parent Coordination

Parent coordination is designed for moderate to high-conflict custody disputes, where one or both parents have demonstrated a consistent unwillingness to comply with court orders. Meant to reduce the conflict and keep children safe, parent coordination is provided by a mental health or legal professional with extensive training and experience in mediation, arbitration, child development, and dealing with high-conflict people. Simply put, the coordinator's job is to help parents implement their court ordered custody plan.

Parents may want to consider parent coordination when, despite a lengthy court process, they can't agree on things such as schedules, overnight visitation, choice of schools, community activities, or drop-offs and pick-ups. A parent coordinator can be especially useful in cases that involve domestic violence, child abuse, drugs, alcohol or situations where one or both parents have a mental illness.

Typically, a parent coordinator is appointed for a period of two years and subsequent periods of the same length, as required. The exact term will be set out in the court order. Most families find two years to be an optimal length of service, because it allows the parent coordinator to fully get to know the family and their issues. It also helps parents avoid having to explain their story to a new mediator or judge over and over again.

After a parent coordinator has been appointed, that person will meet with the parents and the children, as well as review the custody evaluation if one was done, and all other court documents. These preliminary steps help the coordinator to get to know the family. In

53

the early stages (first three to six months), the parent coordinator will meet with the parents/children on a regular basis. Once things are going well, meetings will be scheduled only when a problem arises.

When a dispute occurs, the parent coordinator's job is to help parents: solve their own shared-custody problems, communicate more effectively, incorporate child-development research into parenting styles, and protect the children from the effects of conflict. The coordinator does this by trying to help parents mediate the problem. If that fails, the coordinator has the authority to decide on the issue. Depending on the jurisdiction, decisions are then forwarded to the court and can become legally binding on both parents, often without the need for a court hearing.

For major issues such as a change in legal custody, or a major change in the visitation schedule, the parent coordinator will typically submit a written recommendation to the court. The judge will then review the matter with the parents at a hearing and then make a ruling.

If the coordinator makes a decision that seems wrong or acts in a manner that seems unprofessional to either parent, that parent should first talk with the coordinator about it. If the parent is still unsatisfied, he or she should submit a written complaint to the coordinator, both attorneys (if applicable), and the other parent. The coordinator will then meet with the parent and his or her attorney. If the complaint still can't be resolved, the parent can make a motion to have the parent coordinator removed. A judge will then review the complaint and make a ruling.

If both parents are dissatisfied with the parent coordinator, they can agree to fire that person. However, if only one parent is unhappy, that person cannot fire the coordinator on his/her own. If the parent coordinator feels he/she can no longer help the family, he or she can resign.

Finally, it is important that parents work with a well-trained parent coordinator who adheres to the "Guidelines for Parent Coordination" published by the Association of Family and Conciliation Courts (AFCC) in 2005. This document sets out detailed guidelines regarding ethical obligations and conduct, as well as qualifications for practice including relevant education, training, and experience.

Looking Within

Jared had just turned forty-seven when he walked into my counseling office and confessed that his life had become unmanageable. "I am a compulsive liar. I lie to my wife about everything. She wants me out. I don't blame her. I can't believe I have screwed up my fourth marriage. I love her, I really do. I think there is something wrong with me. Can you help me?" This was a pivotal moment in Jared's life.

Jared had spent much of his adult life chasing happiness. When he visualized being happy he thought of having a beautiful wife, big bank account, nice home, and a fancy car. Yet despite having these things, Jared felt empty inside, and lonely much of the time. His relationships, whether professional or intimate, always seemed to end badly. For a long time he was convinced that it was everyone else who had the problems. He was now beginning to doubt that. He was ready to look within.

***

Now that we have looked at the definition of "win," the stakes, levels of conflict, and the options you have at your finger tips for doing things differently, it is essential that we turn the focus inward. It's time to look within and really learn from the custody fight experience— to use the anger, uncertainty, and sense of loss that is at the heart of every custody battle as a catalyst for personal growth. It's time to look at the most common reasons why parents keep fighting, even when alternatives are staring them in the face.

In his best-seller *Choice Theory: A New Psychology of Personal Freedom*, world-renowned psychiatrist and lecturer William Glasser explains that the human problems we struggle with most, such as abuse, violence, and addiction, are caused by unsatisfying relationships. The suffering, however, is created by ourselves because most of us do a poor job when it comes to establishing and maintaining healthy marriages and friendships. What gets in the way, according to Dr. Glasser, is the illusion that we have control over other people.

Perhaps this strikes you as absurd or radical thinking. But take a moment to think about the role that control has played in your relationship with your ex. Think about the ways in which you and your ex have tried to exert control over each other, both when you were together and since you've split up.

If you think hard enough you will realize most close relationships, at a fundamental level, are an endless pushing and pulling in a struggle for the upper hand. In fact, many of the parents in a difficult custody battle are control junkies seeking a fix at every opportunity. While you may be thinking that sounds a lot like your ex but nothing like you, keep in mind that trying to control others is so common that we often don't realize we are doing it.

One of the best predictors of a healthy, fulfilling and stable marriage is the extent to which both parties feel they are in control of their own destiny. Conversely, one of the best predictors that a relationship will break down is the extent to which one or both people actively try to control the other verbally, physically, or economically. For parents sharing custody, this issue often plays out in terms of unrealistic expectations. To illustrate this, please take a moment and write a list of the expectations you have for your ex. Does your list look anything like this?

My ex will: treat me and my new partner with respect, be fair and honest, regret what he/she put me through, be generous, respect my parenting style, provide emotional support if I need it, answer my calls promptly, and be a good parent and role model for our kids.

If your list looks like mine, you may be in for a long and nasty battle. Why so, when my list seems so perfect? It's unrealistic. If you and your ex couldn't treat each other that way when you were together, what makes you think you can start doing it now? The point is that setting unrealistic expectations for ourselves and our former partners fuels conflict. The question is: Why do we do it in the first place?

Understanding the sense of grief and loss people experience when a relationship ends helps explain why we set unrealistic expectations for ourselves and others. This is clearly explained by Elizabeth Kubler-Ross in her 2005 book *On Grief and Grieving: Finding the Meaning of Grief Through the Five Stages of Loss*. Whenever we lose an important person in our life, says Kubler- Ross, either through divorce, separation or some other way, we go through a five-stage process. The same is true for separation and divorce. The steps are:

Denial. We normally react to an overwhelming incident such as divorce with denial, saying to ourselves things like, "This happens to other people not me," or, "This feels like a bad dream." While denial is a normal way of coping with the emotional overload of a divorce or separation, some people get stuck in this stage for months, even years. These are the same people who at some point stop uttering, "I can't believe this is happening" and begin saying, "I know she/he will come back to me." In healthy scenarios, denial gives way to a broader awareness that change is a normal and healthy part of life.

Anger. Once the reality of the breakup sinks in, denial gives way to anger. In this stage, parents say things to themselves such as, "This is not fair," or "This is all her/his fault." While it's perfectly normal to feel anger in response to a break-up, this stage can be a real test for people who are uncomfortable with powerful emotions, have poor anger control skills, or have a history of violent behavior.

Bargaining. As the anger subsides, we are confronted with feelings of sadness, regret, and a longing to somehow turn back the clock. We summon images of the "good times" and long to return to them, as we try to bargain with our ex, our kids, and our God in a desperate bid to find a way back. During this period it is not uncommon to see one parent get furious with the other one day, and the next send a dinner invitation with flowers and chocolates.

When it becomes clear that all the bargaining in the world isn't going to change things, most people move to level four, the mourning stage. A small percentage, however, go backwards. Those who do, go from sending candy and wanting to reconcile, to hiring an attorney and sending a letter claiming unfit parenting and demanding full custody.

Mourning. Mourning sets in when parents finally realize that the relationship is irrevocably over. This is often when deep feelings of loss, loneliness, and even despair set in. It is not uncommon to want to isolate oneself, have trouble concentrating, and experience problems sleeping soundly.

In the United States, this stage presents a significant challenge because of the tendency of doctors to label those in mourning as having a mental illness, such as depression, and then prescribing medication. For some, the prospect of being labeled mentally ill is so alarming that they choose to struggle through this phase in secrecy. Or worse: they reject the mourning stage altogether and return to the anger phase where they can assume the much more culturally accepted role of the victim who is fighting for what is right and just.

Acceptance. This final stage is marked by understanding, acceptance and peace of mind. We are at this stage when we realize we have worked through and let go of our grievances, resentments and bitterness.

There are five factors that influence how people experience these stages: 1) the form the break-up took (a cordial split or a train wreck),

2) history of domestic violence or substance abuse, 3) the emotional health of the people involved, 4) the extent to which each person has access to supportive and stable friends and family, and 5) whether or not the parents chose to fight things out in court.

The violent father who comes home one day to find a note saying his wife has taken the kids to Brazil, is going to experience grief and loss differently than the mother who mutually agrees with her husband to call it quits. Likewise, an eight-year-old child whose dad disappears from his life will have a much tougher time than a child whose dad moves across the street so he can walk his son to school every day.

It is also important to understand that no one experiences these stages in a purely linear fashion. No one is fully in denial, then absolutely in the anger stage, then immersed in bargaining, and so on. It doesn't work like that. In the course of a day you might wake up with a new bargaining idea, experience denial as you are showering, feel as if you are in acceptance by lunchtime, then slip into anger while watching your ex's favorite show. Just keep in mind that while on this rollercoaster ride of thoughts and feelings, as long as you are processing them in a healthy way you are moving in the right direction.

Understanding how the family court system can undermine the natural healing process is important. With its emphasis on raising the custody stakes, the family law system encourages people to get stuck in an anger and bargaining loop that makes it tough to resolve a dispute. The challenge for parents, once they know about these stages, is to make sure they are not keeping themselves, and everyone else in the family, stuck.

Getting unstuck requires a paradigm shift in our thinking. Instead of seeing your situation as an epic battle that will end with a spectacular courtroom scene where justice prevails, the paradigm shift demands that you begin to see your ex as stuck in one of the five stages of

61

loss (most likely denial, anger or bargaining). The shift in thinking also calls on you to start actively helping your ex get unstuck. Why? Simple, it's in your best interest. The sooner your ex gets to acceptance, the better for everyone involved.

If you think this idea sounds crazy, you are not alone. When I sketch out this concept to parents, a common response is, "You must be nuts. What do I care if my ex ever gets unstuck? I hope he/she rots in hell." Of course, when I hear a parent talk like that the first thought that comes to my mind is "I know which level you are stuck on." The fact is that shifting the way you think about your situation and your ex is at the core of the "new way to win" concept. Custody disputes where both parents are stuck in anger are a mess and seem to never end.

Now that we've looked at grief and loss, it's time to turn to the work we must do in order to get to acceptance. According to Sandra Blakeslee, Julia Lewis and Judith Wallerstein, in *The Unexpected Legacy of Divorce*, separated or divorced parents must complete six critical tasks in order to fully move on. When I see a parent who is stuck in the loss process, it is usually because they are having trouble completing one or more of these tasks.

Ending the Relationship: The first step is all about bringing the relationship to a complete end and, if there are children involved, transitioning to working with your ex to raise the kids in a healthy manner. As we learned earlier, it cannot be overstated how important this stage is when it comes to a child's wellbeing.

Mourning: The end of a relationship is a huge event. It not only affects the parents and children, but also grandparents and other family members, as well as friends. The full dimension of the grief and loss is incalculable. Nevertheless, the mourning must be done so that everyone can move on.

Reclaiming Oneself: "Who am I now that I am divorced? I used to own a home; now I live in a small apartment. I'm here in my body, but I feel lost." Separation and divorce knocks us off balance, and in so doing challenges us to look at ourselves and grapple with the difference between who we were, who we are, and who we want to become. In life we are continually faced with growth opportunities, which we either embrace or turn away from. The task of reclaiming oneself then is really about just that—growing as an individual, becoming stronger, standing in your own light.

Resolving or Containing Intense Emotions: There is perhaps no experience that can overwhelm us emotionally like a break up. This is because separation and divorce has a way of dredging up old unresolved grievances, resentments, and trauma. The result is a buffet of emotions. We must find a way to resolve or move past both the old and new stuff without letting our emotions take over our lives.

Venturing Forth Again: I commonly hear parents say, "I'm done with women," or "I'm done with men, dating and relationships." These folks are living the old adage, "Burn me once, shame on you; burn me twice, shame on me." That's understandable after a painful break up. The challenge now is to work through this—to get past the fear that is at the heart of wanting to avoid relationships.

Now you may be saying, "No problem. I was in a new relationship soon after my break up." Not so fast. Rebound relationships are common, but many are unhealthy, entered into out of a fear of being alone. Venturing forth again is about getting comfortable with uncertainty, about having the courage to learn from your past relationships, about conquering fear.

Rebuilding: The sixth and final task is becoming aware that you are building a new life for yourself and your kids, a life that is better than the old one. And that out of the hardship and struggle of your breakup has emerged healing, wisdom, and peace of mind.

SECTION TWO:

Seven Power Strategies for Ending Your Custody Dispute

Power Strategy #1—Use Power Not Force

Ryan and Fiona had been married eleven years when they separated. The relationship had been rocky, in large part because of Ryan's controlling nature. It didn't help that Ryan was a long-distance truck driver who was away from home twenty days a month. Their nine-year -old son, Dalton, was living with mom full-time. Before going before a judge, both parents had been ordered, by their court-based mediator, to attend a co-parenting class.

In the course of helping Ryan register for my one-day program, he explained that his ex was a stubborn, spiteful, and unreasonable woman. He went on to say:

"If only she would have signed the damn thing, everything would've been better. But she refused. We were at the settlement conference for four hours. I know she felt intimidated, because she can't afford an attorney and the meeting was at my lawyer's office, but, she got the best offer I will ever agree to. If it wasn't for my new wife telling me to compromise, I would never have agreed to offer all that stuff. I'm actually glad she said no. She'll be sorry; my lawyer says the judge will side with me. I just can't get over the fact that she wouldn't sign. I must have asked her twenty-five times in twenty-five different ways. What is wrong with her? If I could have, I would have grabbed her hand and made her sign."

***

There is a big difference between power and force and it is very important to be clear on the difference. In physics, force is defined as any agent that causes a change in the motion of something else. In the world of human relationships, to use force is to compel, constrain, or oblige someone to do something. The frustrated father who is quoted above tried to force his ex to sign a contract, but she refused.

Power, on the other hand, is very different. Power has to come from something or someone. This is where many people confuse power and force, because they assume that the source of real power comes out of the ability or willingness to use force. If this were true, how do we make sense of the power of historic figures such as Mother Teresa, Martin Luther King, Mahatma Gandhi, and Nelson Mandela? These people used power to change the course of history in the face of overwhelming force.

True power is based in such universal principles as justice, compassion, honesty, integrity, and respect. Power inspires us, lifts us up, energizes, and feeds our soul. It does not need to be justified. Force, by contrast, draws its strength in relation to things it can move or act against. Force is coercive, something that needs to be explained, defended, and protected. Force is about winning and losing.

When Nelson Mandela was released from jail in 1990, he was more powerful than the South African apartheid regime that had put him behind bars because his power was built on universal principles. When Mahatma Gandhi walked 241 miles barefoot to non-violently protest British control of India, he was more powerful than the entire British army. When Martin Luther King gave his famous, "I have a dream" speech in Washington, he was more powerful than the Jim Crow legacy of slavery and all of the police dogs and water cannons that had been used against civil rights marchers.

In 1950, when Mother Teresa set up The Missionaries of Charity, her goal was to love and care for those people in the world nobody else was prepared to look after. With no money—just an abiding faith in the essential goodness of human beings—she built a global movement that empowered and lifted out of poverty millions of people all over the world. Mother Teresa was more powerful than the brutal and cruel forces of poverty, because like the many famous and anonymous people before and since, her power came out of her alignment with universal principles.

As you reflect on what the next steps in your custody dispute will be, consider what might have happened had the mother in the previous example given in and signed the custody plan after her ex's twenty-fifth request. I suspect the father would have left the settlement conference thinking he had "won." He might even have bragged to his friends that he had forced his ex to sign. Mom, on the other hand, would probably have been kicking herself for signing something she wasn't comfortable with. Then, if she is like most co-parents who are forced into an agreement they are unhappy with, she would eventually stop following it and want it changed.

This gets to the heart of how power and force are different in custody situations. Coercing someone to "sign" produces a weak contract, not an agreement. Like bad used cars, weak contracts are the ones that breakdown over and over. Many parents fail to recognize, that it is in the self-interest of both parties to ensure they develop a mutually beneficial agreement and not simply a binding contract. Having at least one parent go into the process from a position of power is the key to making that happen.

***

Ryan and Fiona eventually attended my co-parenting program. At the end of the class, Fiona stayed behind. She explained that the day after their unsuccessful settlement conference, Ryan had left her a voice message saying she was an unfit parent and that he intended to go to trial and get 100 percent custody of their son. Three days after that, she got a letter from his attorney saying that Ryan would also be asking the judge to order Fiona to pay all of his lawyer's fees. Frightened by these threats, Fiona asked her parents to pay for an attorney, and they agreed.

The first issue up for consideration when they went to court was Ryan's request that Fiona pay his legal fees. Despite reassurance from her lawyer that the judge would never approve such a request, she was scared. Unemployed at the time and living with her parents, she had no idea how she would come up with that kind of money. With a smile, Fiona explained what happened next.

The judge called on Ryan's lawyer to explain why Fiona should pay for his fees. The judge listened with a stern look on his face. Then to Fiona's surprise, he let out a deep belly laugh. The kind that is infectious. His laugh was so unexpected, everyone in the room smiled, except for Ryan and his attorney. The request was denied.

Fiona's attorney then asked the judge to order a child-custody evaluation. This was appropriate, she claimed, because it would include a psychiatric evaluation of both parents, and show whether or not Ryan had mental health problems. Ryan's attorney strongly objected. The judge not only agreed to Fiona's request, he went a step further, and ordered Ryan to pay for the full six-thousand-dollar evaluation.

***

Power Strategy #2—Unlocking the Power of Intention

Veronica had felt paralyzed since the father of her children walked out on her. High school sweethearts, she had always thought they would be holding hands on the beach when they were in their eighties. Losing him after fourteen years of being together shook her deeply. Previously a confident and well grounded full-time mom, Veronica felt as if she were in a row boat lost at sea. Unable to pay the mortgage, she moved her young family in with her parents.

The kids loved living with their grandparents. Within a month of moving in, their school grades were up and they were laughing more. While Veronica was relieved to see her kids doing well, she felt as if she were sinking. Unsure of how to help herself, she retreated into a life of television shows, long naps, and nervous pacing. Veronica desperately wanted to hold on to her old life. She knew she should be looking for a job, or going back to school, or something, but these things felt beyond her. Veronica was stuck between a past that she didn't want to let go of, and a future that she didn't want to start thinking about.

Veronica's parents encouraged her at every step. They recommended counseling, exercise, healthy eating, and going to church. They understood that she was struggling through the most difficult period in her life. One afternoon while watching the *Oprah* show with her mom, Veronica's life changed. The show featured the movie *The Secret*. Veronica was introduced, for the first time, to the law of attraction and the power of intention. Later that evening she sat down with a sketch pad and began mapping out a plan for her future.

71

...eral days later when I met with Veronica in my counseling office, something was noticeably different about her. It seemed as though a weight had been lifted from her shoulders. She confided in me that God was steering her towards healing, and providing the tools needed to rebuild her life. She cited as evidence having had an "aha moment" while watching Oprah. Learning about the power of intention at exactly this moment in her life, she explained, was no coincidence. I agreed.

***

Intention, or purpose, is about focusing, aspiring, and planning. In business schools, first year students are taught about the importance of vision when starting a new company. A venture must begin with a clear and well-thought-out mental image of what the company will be and where it will go once it is open for business.

Too often parents in custody disputes lack a clear set of intentions, saying simply that they are doing "what is best" for the kids. When I ask parents what they mean by that, most say that everything will get better when the other parent changes. It is precisely because of this lack of vision that most businesses fail within their first or second year of operation.

The key to unlocking the power of intention is to put in place a positive, detailed and written vision of what things will look like when (not if) the dispute is resolved. Setting clear intentions will help you get away from hoping, pleading, forcing, and simply wishing that everything will magically get better. The following five steps will help you get started.

Step One – Complete a Quality World Inventory

William Glasser, in his book *Choice Theory*, explains that every person has a "quality world." Similar to a cherished photo album, our quality world is where we store the pictures we have of the people, things, and systems of belief that are most important to us. These pictures are directly linked to our wellbeing, because they are not just mementos; they represent our vision of the good life, of how to meet our basic human needs for: survival, freedom, power, belonging, and fun.

If a picture in our quality world is meeting one or more of our needs, we will leave it in the album. If, however, a picture stops working for us, we will take the picture out and insert a more satisfying replacement. For example, if you were married, on your wedding day you probably had a picture of you and your ex living together happily in your quality world. Given that the relationship didn't work out, it is safe to say that at some point, one or both of you will remove that picture from your quality world.

Sometimes we leave a picture in our quality world even though it no longer serves us to do so. This behavior is typical of someone who chooses to stay with a partner long after the relationship has irrevocably soured. Take for instance the woman who remains with her violent partner. In her quality world, she may have a picture of the smiling and loving person she married, not the enraged, stumbling drunk he later became. She may want to leave, but finds herself struggling against a vision of how her relationship was supposed to be, the vision imprinted on her quality world picture.

Releasing a quality world picture that we want to hold on to is painful, because it means letting go of the dreams we once had. Taking your wedding picture out of your quality world is hard. Removing your picture of an intact and happy family is hard. But so is holding on to them. Replacing these pictures, however, can mean the difference between moving forward and getting stuck in the first three levels of the grief and loss process: denial, anger, and bargaining.

I wish I could tell you there is a delete button you could press, or a recipe you could use, to tidy up your quality world. There isn't. The closest thing I know of to a formula for reluctantly taking a picture out of your quality world is in striving for broader awareness and balance.

You also need to make sure you avoid telling yourself that the custody problems you are having are beyond repair. The key to doing this is changing the way you interpret and respond to events in your life. You can do this either by using the coping tools that once helped you through a stressful situation, or by finding new stress-reduction tools.

Step Two – Find Stillness

In his book *Full Catastrophe Living: Using the Wisdom of Your Body and Mind to Face Stress, Pain and Illness*, Jon Kabat-Zinn explains that the key to managing stress is mindfulness. Mindfulness, says Kabat-Zinn, is "paying attention in a particular way, on purpose, in the present moment, non-judgmentally." Mindfulness is easy to learn, costs nothing, and has been proven in countless university studies to be extraordinarily effective at helping people find internal balance.

Mindfulness allows you to tap inner resources that will help you move beyond your suffering toward happiness and calm. It helps you to develop a new way of interpreting and responding to the events in your life. This approach is grounded in concepts such as acceptance, patience, and letting go.

Unfortunately, many Westerners are leery of concepts such as mindfulness, which they perceive as too New-Age or too passive. They couldn't be farther from the truth. Practiced for centuries, mindfulness is one of the most powerful ways known for achieving and maintaining balance.

Step Three – Move Beyond Blame and Guilt

To fully unlock the power of intention, parents need to remove the blame and guilt that keeps them focused on the past instead of on visualizing the future they want.

We have all seen a homeless person pushing a shopping cart full of garbage. What about two carts, the poor fellow pushing one and pulling the other? You, with your unresolved issues and mixed feelings, are not unlike this unfortunate person. On one hand you feel the pull of those things you did or said that you wish you could take back, while, on the other hand, you feel the push of bitterness and resentment. How much garbage are you pushing and pulling around? Are you one of the lucky ones with only a few items in the cart, or do you have two carts and still they are overflowing? If you are like most parents in a custody dispute, you feel like you are pushing at least one cart.

Of course the problem with pushing around a shopping cart full of unresolved junk is that it gets between you and your future. It weighs you down. Most parents would rather walk on hot coals than try to clean out their cart. Just the thought of reaching into the cart is enough to give some people a feeling of panic. If you think deeply about it, this too is confusing, because the garbage in the cart is from the past and is therefore harmless. Still, the emotions we attach to the past can live on and cause no end of misery in the present, if we let them.

Much like removing an old picture from our quality world, we must commit ourselves to not letting the wreckage of our past dominate our future. As difficult as that may seem, I can assure you that pushing around that cart for the rest of your life will be much harder. The only sensible choice we have is to let go.

Step Four – Tend Your Spiritual Garden
Parents frequently tell me that because of a custody battle, they have stopped going to church, synagogue, the mosque, or the lake where they once liked to meditate. If you have an interrupted relationship with your higher power, it is time to address your spiritual needs and recommit to that relationship.

Never underestimate the power of prayer. During difficult times, don't limit yourself to the options that you are able to conceive of alone. Seek counsel from your higher power. When you do so, reach out with an open mind. Allow your higher power to inspire in you a new level of understanding, and a renewed sense of hopefulness. Have faith and the solutions you seek will be revealed.

Step Five – Tap into the Science of Happiness
Happiness is not a commodity that can be bought, sold, or traded. Happiness is also not the same as pleasure. Rather, it is an inner resource that needs to be cultivated. This concept confuses some people, because they don't understand the difference between pleasure and happiness.

Gambling, drinking wine, great sex, winning a soccer game, or getting a promotion, are examples of things that may give us pleasure. None of these things, however, can make us happy. This is because happiness is rooted in such things as a purposeful life, parenthood, integrity, compassion, and caring relationships.

This makes sense when you ponder why some people are happy most of the time, while others seem chronically miserable. Our general mood or disposition, it turns out, is in part determined by what we value. According to the research, a life focused on the acquisition of money and power alone, is unlikely to result in happiness.

Once we realize that winning the lottery isn't going to make us authentically happy, we are freed up to shift our attention to those things that can. The good news is that everyone is capable of being happier, if they are willing to learn how. According to Sonja Lyubomirsky, in *The How of Happiness: A New Approach to Getting the Life You Want*, happiness comes from: practicing gratitude, nurturing healthy relationships, learning to let go, living in the moment, taking care of ourselves, and better managing the stress and trauma of living in the modern world.

***

Within a few weeks of watching the *Oprah* episode on the power of intention, Veronica had begun to see her custody dispute differently. Rather than a tragic story of loss and betrayal, she had come to see the end of her marriage as a critical step in her growth as a human being. Looking back, she realized that somewhere in her marriage she had lost herself. A freedom-loving and confident person when she got married, she had become dependant on her husband for her happiness and sense of direction.

While Veronica was still very angry at her ex-husband, she had begun working on forgiveness. Interestingly, she realized that the more she worked on her self, the easier it was to forgive him. Visualizing and mapping out her future, especially her new co-parenting relationship with her ex-husband, helped her to feel stronger and more alive than she had in years.

During one of our last counseling sessions, Veronica told me that she had learned to be more grateful for the blessings in her life, and to live more in the moment. She had also adopted a mantra that she would whisper when she found herself preoccupied with either her past or her future. Her mantra was: "May I meet this moment fully. May I meet it as a friend."

***

Power Strategy #3—Build Your Kids a Safe Harbor

Grace was sixteen when she went to live with her maternal grandparents permanently. Life with her parents had been hard. Their marriage had been an on-again off-again affair that had taken many sudden turns. After they broke up, Grace bounced back and forth from one to the other for five years. Rather than getting better, however, things got much worse.

To Grace, the war over her made no sense. She wanted to be with her mom and her dad, to love them both. Being asked to choose sides made her sad and angry at the same time. It also made her want to cut herself. She didn't want to die, but desperately wanted the pain inside to go away. Unfortunately, rather than help their daughter, her parents blamed each other for causing her problems.

Grace was relieved when the court granted her request to move in with her grandparents. She had explained to the judge that they loved her in a way that her parents were unable to. They refused to take sides. She felt safe with them, cared for, protected.

***

Raising healthy, happy, and resilient kids, despite separation or divorce, is a challenge. It is difficult for many reasons, some of which parents have control over and some of which they don't. Research tells us that it isn't the breakup, as much as how parents behave after separation or divorce that determines how kids fare in life.

The best way to ensure that your children will turn out for the best is to: build them a safe harbor, insulate them from the dispute, and reassure them through your demeanor, words, and actions that they are important and loved by both parents. I like to tell parents in my workshops they can fight with their ex until they are on social security, but unless they want their kids to turn out upside down, they need to actively keep them out of the custody fray.

In an amicable separation or divorce, building a safe harbor is easy. In cases with more conflict, it takes power. The following three steps will provide you with the foundation to protect your children from the toxic side-effects of your custody dispute.

Step One—Help them Cope with the Emotional Rollercoaster

When it comes to separation or divorce, kids experience many of the same emotions as adults. Feelings of anxiety and fear, denial, anger, confusion, guilt, and deep sadness can overwhelm children when a custody dispute drags on or when parents involve them in a dispute inappropriately. These emotions can lead to serious problems.

Anxiety and fear: Like any trauma that results in the loss of an important person in our lives, separation and divorce can produce fear of abandonment. In children's minds, if one parent can send the other away for being "bad," does that mean they could also be sent away if they don't behave? Other concerns can also surface in children, such as those related to money, school, the dark, and illness. Younger, anxious, and fearful children will show this by being clingier than usual, wanting to sleep with mom or dad, or wetting the bed. Older kids may start having stomach aches at school, tend to isolate or stay home more, complain about having trouble sleeping, and they may be generally more irritable.

Anger: No matter how bad the relationship, most kids hope their parents will work things out and stay together. When that doesn't happen it can provoke a great deal of anger, which, depending on the kinds of supports in place and the child's ability to manage powerful emotions, can be very overwhelming. Having to move, change schools, make new friends, change soccer teams, and see the non-residential parent much less than they want to, can also fuel feelings of anger.

Confusion: Kids often wonder how life will be different at Mom's new house or Dad's new apartment. Will the rules be the same? Will there be more chores? Will I have to share a room with my new step-sister? To help your kids put their concerns to rest, it's important to help them adjust to the changes in their lives as quickly as possible.

Guilt: An astonishing number of children believe they caused their parents to split up (e.g. Mom and Dad were always fighting about my school grades). Many also assume that they are the reason their parents can't get along after the breakup (e.g. if it weren't for me they wouldn't have to see each other and get into all those fights). A simple way to address this issue is to consistently remind your children that they are not responsible for your breakup or for the ongoing conflict. Reassure them that these are adult issues and that things are going to get better.

Deep sadness: Children go through the same fives stages of loss and grief as adults. They also have a quality world with pictures they do not want to let go of. When they realize the breakup is real and permanent it is normal for them to struggle with deep sadness. Signs to watch for include: poor sleep, difficulty concentrating, loss of motivation, irritability, changes in eating habits, a negative self-image, and feeling unlovable. The good news is that, in normal cases, feelings of deep sadness are short-lived. In fact, as matters are worked out, the child should emerge on the other side of this stage more resilient than before.

81

Whether or not your children share these feelings with you will have a lot to do with the kind of relationship you have with them. Should you decide to pursue counseling as a way of helping your child through any of these difficult emotions, it is critical that:

- *Both parents are involved.* A parent should not keep the fact that a child is in counseling a secret. Ideally, both parents should be actively involved. If one parent cannot attend in person, accommodation should be made so that he or she can participate by speaker phone.

- *Work with an expert in post-separation and divorce adjustment.* Whether a psychologist, marriage therapist, clinical social worker, pastoral, or some other type of counselor, it is important to engage a professional who specializes in this area. Most therapists will say they do, but not all have the extensive formal training and experience needed. You can get a list of questions to ask a prospective counselor on www. ANewWaytoWin.com.

   The High Conflict Institute has developed a brief counseling program for families struggling through a separation or divorce. *New Ways for Families*, teaches parents to focus on making positive changes and avoid becoming preoccupied with defending themselves in an endless "attack-defend" cycle. Both parents and the children participate in this twelve-session program. More information is available at www. NewWays4Families.com.

- *Don't ask for court reports.* As soon as you start asking a therapist to do more than confirm attendance in a letter to the court, you are potentially undermining the process. When your child realizes that what is said in a counseling session may be introduced by one parent in family court, the counseling process ceases to be a safe place for the child to speak openly and honestly. The sessions may continue to appear fruitful, but they will in fact have turned into a meaningless exercise that has more to do with the child trying to avoid getting into trouble with either parent, than anything else.

- *Get a second opinion before starting your child on mental health medications.* In our quick-fix society, it can seem that mental health medicines are the "go to" solution anytime someone is unhappy or having a hard time. I often hear of well-meaning therapists who lack expertise in child custody cases, diagnosing a child with a serious mental illness shortly after starting with a case. The diagnosis often includes the recommendation that the parents consult with a doctor and start the child on psychotropic medications. Then, after three months, when the child has made no progress in counseling (in large part because the therapist is in over his/her head), the parents are told that the child is resistant to talk therapy and they are encouraged to focus more on drug-based treatment.

  If you are thinking about starting your child on mental health medications, or perhaps, you are wondering if your child should continue on psychotropic medications, please read, *Should You Medicate Your Child's Mind?* by Dr. Elizabeth Roberts, a board-certified child and adolescent psychiatrist.

Step Two – Keep the Kids out of the Middle

An essential component of building children a safe harbor is keeping them out of the middle of adult disputes. This is easier said than done, especially if your ex is playing dirty. Parents can, without realizing it, involve the children in their breakup in many unintended ways. When this happens the child is put in an uncomfortable position and asked, often in very subtle ways, to choose sides.

Building your children a safe harbor requires that you avoid the unwitting behavior that entwines children in the custody process. Here are some of the most common ways parents put their children in the middle:

Undermining your child's relationship with the other parent: Saying or doing things that undermine the child's relationship with your ex can be harmful. Avoiding this pitfall can be tricky, especially in situations where it is important to be honest with your child. For example, if the other parent misses a visit and fails to call, it is best to reassure the child that the absent parent is okay and that missing a visit does not mean the parent does not love the child. Then, when the child is out of earshot, calmly contact the other parent by phone or e-mail and find out what happened. The point here is not to speak negatively about the other parent's irresponsible behavior. While it may be perfectly reasonable to feel your ex has behaved poorly, telling that to your child will only make a bad situation worse.

Seeking revenge: Using a child as a pawn or a tool for exacting revenge on your ex is highly inappropriate. A child should never be used in this way. If you are out for revenge, remember that such behavior is likely to be very harmful to your children and get you in serious trouble. If you find yourself acting in this way, you should find a good therapist and work through the feelings at the core of the problem.

Using your child as a spy. Asking children to be your eyes and ears while they are with the other parent is not okay. While it is perfectly all right to ask such questions as, "How was your weekend?" or "Why did you throw that tantrum I heard about?" it is inappropriate to ask children questions with regard to your ex's personal or professional life. If you have such questions, put them to your ex yourself.

Using your child as a therapist: The early stages of a separation or divorce can be a lonely and emotionally volatile time for parents. Putting your child in the role of therapist, relying on your child for

84

support, reassurance, and guidance, isn't healthy for either of you. Sometimes parents do this without realizing it, and other times the child will initiate this behavior, but, in either case, it is unhealthy.

Involving the child in money issues: Money is one of the most common things parents fight about, and one of the most common ways that children get drawn into their parents' disputes. Talking with children about child or spousal support, or asking them to deal with the other parent on any kind of money issue, is unfair and very uncomfortable for the child. Children are rarely the cause of their parents' money troubles. That said, they often come to equate the payment of child support with their parents' willingness to love and take care of them. Regardless of your financial issues, keeping the child clear of them is essential.

Allowing kids to refuse visitation: In the initial stages of a separation or divorce it is not uncommon for a young child to resist going to stay with the non-residential parent. Told, for example, that they must stay with Daddy for the weekend, they may fuss, cry, or throw a tantrum. This is usually more about age-based attachment issues than anything else. Teens will also sometimes express reluctance to stay with the non-residential parent, because they would rather hang out with their friends, among other reasons.

In some cases, a parent will misinterpret this resistance as being the result of a smear campaign on the part of the other parent. In most situations this is not the case, and the very act of making such an allegation escalates the custody dispute considerably. The situation is made worse when one or both parents let the kids decide whether they spend time with the other parent. This puts children in the unenviable position of having to choose one parent over the other. If a child is reluctant to stay with either parent, the family should work with a specialist to find ways to resolve the issue.

Making community events high drama: If you and your ex can't be in the same room together without drama, don't be in the same room together. The way to do this is to set up a detailed schedule of birthdays, school programs, soccer games, performances, and holidays and stick to it.

Communicating with your ex through your child: Enlisting your child as a "FedEx" courier to convey messages puts them in the middle. Communicating with your ex should be done directly, parent to parent, by e-mail, text, or telephone.

Avoid doing pick-ups and drop-offs at a police station: Establishing the local police station as a drop-off/pick-up point is not uncommon. In fact, you may have already done so. This is a bad idea, because it doesn't work. This procedure is often suggested when parents cannot keep from arguing during child transfers. The idea is that if they transfer a child in front of a police station, they will behave properly. However, parents who want to argue will do it front of a police station, McDonalds, or during an audience with the pope, for that matter.

The other reason not to use a police station as a transfer spot is that it sends kids the ominous message about how safe it is to be with mom and dad. You are saying to your kids that when both parents are around, they are only secure if a cop is there too. The point is that building a safe harbor is all about making choices that remove worry, fear, and uncertainty from the child's mind. Choosing to do transfers at the police station, especially given how ineffective it is, is likely to make things worse, not better.

It is essential to keep in mind that a child can only be in the middle if both parents allow it. If one parent refuses to allow it, the child cannot get entangled. Imagine two parents and a child playing a skipping game called "kid in the middle." If one parent drops the rope and refuses to keep playing the game there is no way for the child to remain in the middle. It's the same in a custody battle. If your ex plays games that involve your child inappropriately, by choosing not to play along you have taken a powerful step toward protecting your child.

Step Three – Nurture Resilience

The final component in creating a safe harbor is nurturing resilience. Some kids are like the old kids' toy called the Weebles, which "wobble but they don't fall down." However, many are like a porcelain vase that, when it drops, shatters into a million pieces. A range of excellent resources are available to parents who want to nurture resilience in their children.

One is a book by Martin Seligman, entitled *The Optimistic Child: A Proven Program to Safeguard Children Against Depression and Build Lifelong Resilience*. This book offers parents a structured program for teaching their children how to use the power of optimism to be more successful academically, athletically, and socially.

The second resource, developed by the Search Institute, based in Minneapolis, Minnesota, is called the *40 Development Assets*. Focused on how to help children grow up to be self-reliant, these assets provide parents with a road map for how to raise emotionally healthy children.

The assets are divided up into eight categories: support, empowerment, boundaries and expectations, constructive use of time, commitment to learning, positive values, social competencies, and positive identify. The Search Institute Web site, offers parents free step-by-step instructions for how to instill these important assets in children ages 3–5, 5–8, 9–12 and 12–18.

According to their Web site (www.search-institute.org): "Studies of more than 2.2 million young people in the United States consistently show that the more assets young people have, the less likely they are to engage in a wide range of high-risk behaviors, and the more likely they are to thrive. Assets have power for all young people, regardless of their gender, economic status, family, or race/ethnicity. Furthermore, levels of assets are better predictors of high-risk involvement and thriving than poverty or being from a single-parent family."

Finally, in my workshops, I regularly encourage parents to use the 40 Development Assets as a neutral framework for setting parenting goals. Everyone wants their children to grow up to be strong and resilient; using these assets as a guideline can help.

Power Strategy #4—Master the Art of Shared Custody Aikido

Whether or not a problem gets worked out quickly or blows up into an ugly court battle, often depends on how skilled the parents are at assertively and constructively managing disagreement. The ancient martial art of aikido offers an understanding into managing conflict, in our lives as well as in custody disputes. A Japanese term that means, "Way of Harmonious Spirit," aikido stresses the importance of working through conflicts in a way that promotes harmony, balance, and peace of mind.

When attacked, an aikido master blends with the energy of the opponent and redirects the attack, instead of opposing it with brute force. This approach is built on the belief that there is no need to fear conflict, as it is a part of everyday life. When confronted, move out of the way. Rather than challenging your attacker, channel the person's energy in a way that restores balance. Embrace the path of least effort.

Now you may be saying to yourself this all sounds fine, but you don't have the time, the energy or the money to attend aikido classes. Don't despair; you don't need to. In the 1990s, some clever business people adapted the principles of aikido to solve customer-related problems. The same principles were then picked up by police, who adapted them to handle aggressive people. They called their adaptation "verbal aikido." I have modified the verbal aikido concept for use in difficult child custody situations.

89

SHARED CUSTODY AIKIDO

Building on the principles that are ground the martial art, this form of verbal aikido calls on you to make the following commitments:

1. The best way to respond to force is with power. I am at ease leading by example, as my kids need me to.

2. I will align my dealings with my ex to the principle of least effort. In so doing, I will refuse to run in circles, pace endlessly, or spend hours figuring out what I wish I would have said.

3. When a shared-custody conflict issue arises, I won't over-react or inflame the situation by responding too quickly.

4. Rather than make assumptions about the problem, I will ask for clarification. Rather than assigning blame, I will accept responsibility. Rather than making accusations, I will focus on solutions.

5. Before responding I will pause, center myself, and fully regain my equilibrium. I will remind myself that I have not always responded well in the past and commit to doing better.

6. My response will channel the energy of the problem in a direction that is productive, positive, and healthy, for me, my kids, and my ex.

7. I will remind myself on an ongoing basis that I am making the right choices. When my children are happy adults, I will be secure in knowing that I took the high road.

These principles provide a road map for how to engage a difficult ex in a calmly-assertive way that is neither aggressive nor passive. Parents using these principles feel comfortable speaking their minds, but they do so in a way that shows respect for others. They know that when interacting with others; tone, body language, and eye contact are as important as words. They also recognize that certain behaviors are more likely to cause anger and should be avoided. These include making demands, threats, and accusations, as well as name calling, interrogating, criticizing, blaming, and condemning.

Shared custody aikido encourages the use of "I" statements rather than "you" statements. For instance, a parent would say by phone or by e-mail: "I worry when you are late to pick up Ryan. He hasn't complained, but I'm sure he feels hurt. If you know you are going to be late, please call and tell him." The same communication done in the form of a "you" doesn't work quite as well: "Why are you always late? Do you know how that makes Ryan feel? How would you feel in his place? You would feel that your father doesn't love you anymore. You could at least send a text message if you are going to be late."

In both cases the words used conveyed the same message. But whereas the "you" message was aggressive and even accusatory, the "I" approach was distinctly subtle and polite, while still being direct. Using the "I" approach is essential, especially when dealing with overly sensitive and defensive people.

This form of verbal aikido also helps parents transition to using a business-like approach in the way they share custody. As mentioned earlier in the section regarding the two types of shared-custody plans, the higher-conflict *parallel plan*, asks parents to use a business-like approach with each other. To illustrate this point, consider the following example.

Imagine you work at a call center of a large company such as IBM or Apple. Day in and day out you hear non-stop complaints from angry and frustrated people. If you were to communicate with customers the way parents in a custody dispute often talk to each other, it might

91

sound like this: "Do we have to go over this again? You are a pain in my *%$#&, you know that? Stop calling me and complaining all the time!" Click. While we all feel like saying such things to a customer sometimes, we don't, because it would only make matters worse.

Now let's imagine this same person used shared custody aikido skills in dealing with his complaining ex. The conversation might sound like this: "I can see why you are concerned. I want to work out the problem for the sake of the kids. I also don't want things to fester or blow up, for your sake as well as mine." When this kind of disarming approach is used consistently, the shared-custody relationship slowly transitions towards harmony and balance.

When I explain this concept in my workshops, some parents show a lot of resistance. I often hear, "I have used that approach before, but nothing works with my ex." Yet when I dig in and ask how that parent applied the principles and how her/his ex responded, a telling picture emerges. What I typically find out is that both parents work and are successful in their jobs. That over the years they were both hotheads from time to time and at least a couple times, things got ugly. Then the relationship ended badly and at least one parent got a pit-bull attorney. When I ask for an example of how they have been using the aikido principles, most parents switch from saying "I tried them—they don't work" to "I have sort of tried them."

The other response I get is something like, "Strong people don't wave white flags." They see the shared custody aikido approach as akin to surrender. They are more comfortable doing things their way, as they always have. Of course, the problem is, that "their way" got them stuck. When I hear parents talk like that, I picture the energizer bunny marching up against a wall, going nowhere until the batteries run out. Behind the bunny I see two exhausted little kids praying quietly for their mom and dad. Praying that, soon, all the fighting will stop.

I try and break through the resistance these parents show by fr
the issue in terms of self-interest. The truth is that the shared (
aikido approach is very effective at getting people what they w
especially when they are up against a chronically angry ex. Th
because the aikido approach helps both parents get their needs met.
The calmly assertive parent is able to communicate openly, directly,
and confidently without feeling steamrolled. The angry parent feels
listened to and engaged in a respectful manner.

Using aikido skills with an angry ex takes practice and patience. Here
are some tips on how to do it well:

Stay in balance. When you begin to feel angry, or sense that your ex is,
step away from the interaction. Whether you are talking face-to-face
or on the phone, corresponding by e-mail or text, politely end the
exchange and wait until you cool down before you resume. Take the
time you need, whether that is a few minutes or a couple of days. This
will give you both a chance to regain your balance.

Focus on relaxing. While taking a break to reduce anger, try doing
some deep breathing, counting backwards, or visualizing waves or a
sunset. These kinds of proven relaxation techniques can quickly help
you gain a sense of calmness and the ability to focus.

Visualize the problem. Once you have regained balance, it is time to
look at the problem and see what options there are for resolving it.
This will keep you from jumping to conclusions or speaking rashly.
Perhaps ask a friend or family member for their perspective on your
problem before moving forward.

Look at how you are communicating. Are you being too passive or too
assertive? Are you using "I" statements or "you" statements? Are you
monitoring the intangible aspects of communication, such as tone and
body language? Ask yourself if there is some way to communicate your
message more effectively.

Consider injecting a little humor. Taking things too seriously can fuel conflict. Inserting a little self-deprecating or silly humor into a conversation can be very disarming. Just remember not to make your ex the target of a joke or sarcastic remark.

Document your interaction. You may want to finish your discussion by e-mail, which often promotes well-considered, business-like communication. If this doesn't help – for example if your ex tends to send hostile e-mail – remember that you don't have to respond in the same manner. Take your time and formulate a measured response using the techniques of shared-custody verbal aikido. Always remember to keep copies of your e-mail communications so you can show them to a judge if needed.

Shared-Custody Aikido in Action
Reading about these concepts and using them in real life are two different things. To help you begin applying the aikido approach in your situation, this section features a series of low-to high-conflict exchanges where one parent is using the shared custody aikido approach.

Low- to Moderate-Conflict Issues: When dealing with low- to moderate-conflict issues, it is important to think carefully about which form of communication (in-person, phone, text, or e-mail) is best suited to the issue. Remember that even if an exchange starts face-to-face or on the phone, it's okay to pause and then switch to e-mail.

That's a Bad Idea
Your ex: "That plan will never work. We tried something like that already, and it didn't work out."
Aikido Response: "You may be right. Perhaps we could try to modify the plan. Any suggestions on how we could do that so it will work for all of us?

Fairness

Your ex: "Asking me to pay for gym clothes is totally unfair"
Aikido Response: "I know I expect too much sometimes, but I'm not sure I'm being unfair in this case. Anyway, I'm glad you brought it up, and we should discuss it. Help me understand how you are feeling?"

Listening

Your ex: "You never listen to a word I say. I just explained to you why I can't change my vacation to July. I already bought the tickets."
Aikido Response: "If I understand correctly, you bought tickets and want to take the kids to Portugal over the holidays, when I thought I would take them to visit my parents. Did you forget that I'd made plans? Anyway, let me think about it and get back to you. I'm not saying it is okay, but I will think about it."

The Bad Guy

Your ex: "It seems like no matter what I do, it's never good enough. I am always the bad guy."
Aikido response: "I don't think you are the bad guy all the time. But sometimes I get frustrated with you, as I know you do with me. When something you do really bugs me, I want to be able to say so. I want you to be open with me too, okay?

Higher-Conflict Issues: I recommend that you consider using only e-mail for your discussions with a higher-conflict ex. Also remember to keep copies of these interactions. That way, you create a paper trail you can go to if you ever need to look back over what's been said.

A Bruise

Your ex: "I can't believe you are accusing me of hitting my own child."
Aikido response: "I'm not saying you did, I'm just repeating what Amy told me. She showed me a bruise on her leg and said that you hit her, because she wouldn't finish her dinner. Can you please tell me what happened?"

Visitation Resistance

Your ex: "This is bull. We always have a great time together. This is your doing."

Aikido response: "I'm as concerned as you are. It's very important to me that Brian spends as much time with his dad as possible. I'm not sure why he is saying this, but I know he misses his friends on weekends. Maybe he's mad at you for some reason. I suggest that we both talk with him and follow up with each other by Wednesday. How does that sound?

Restraining Order

Your ex: "I would never take her to see that creep. I have told you that over and over."

Aikido response: "I am asking because of a disturbing picture Sierra drew in school yesterday. The teacher was concerned and asked who the people in the drawing were. Sierra said one was her and the other was her grandfather. I asked her when she last saw your father and she said she sees him all the time. I know you wouldn't put our daughter at risk, not after what that man did to you. Still, I have to take this seriously. I would like you to help me figure out what is going on here. Do you have contact with your father when Sierra is with you?

Parental Alienation

Your ex: "You are alienating me from my son with all the disparaging comments you make. Now he says he wants to live with you full-time. My lawyer says this sounds like a case of parental alienation."

Aikido response: "I can sense from your e-mail that you are very upset. Before writing this reply, I had a talk with Robert and told him his time with you is very important to all of us. He knows that. I just think he's getting tired of that two-hour train ride twice a week. He'll have to learn to live with that. Of more concern to me, though, is that you believe I am speaking negatively about you. You and I don't see eye to eye on a lot of things, but I would never discuss our problems with our son or say anything that would interfere with his relationship with you. I'd like to get to the bottom of this right away. I suggest that we both speak with Robert's therapist about it and get his help working it out. How does that sound?

Finally, while reading the above examples, you may have found yourself whispering, "This would never work." What is your alternative? Perhaps you have already tried a civilized approach, but it failed because your ex prefers to throw gas. Shared Custody Aikido offers you a power-based way to put out fires. While you may struggle a little as you get comfortable with using this approach, you have nothing to lose by trying it. The more frequently you do so, the better you will get at it.

Power Strategy #5—Learn to Negotiate with Difficult People

Most parents I meet don't like to negotiate, even at a garage sale. And they certainly don't want to negotiate with their ex, because it has always gone badly in the past. For these people, the act of getting a lawyer is as much about wanting someone to negotiate for them as any other reason.

Negotiating shared custody problems doesn't have to be intimidating or complicated. Once you learn what style of negotiation best suits you, and begin using the four rules of negotiation sketched out in this chapter, the prospect of negotiating will never frighten you again.

WHAT TYPE OF SHARED-CUSTODY NEGOTIATOR ARE YOU?

Everyone has their own way of working through a shared-custody impasse or conflict. Some people jump in with both feet, while others hate negotiating and will stop at almost nothing to avoid it. Then there is everybody else who falls somewhere in between the two extremes.

The hard negotiator is a very difficult parent to deal with. This negotiating style is difficult to work with because it is marked by:
- A need to win at all costs
- Willingness to lie, cheat, and mislead to gain advantage

- A need to control and a tendency to view the other parent as the enemy
- Seeing things in black and white—a "my way or the highway" mentality
- A focus on blaming others
- Making a lot of demands and a reluctance to make concessions

Hard negotiators have often learned their skills in the business world or the military, and bring the skill set learned in those arenas to bear on the task of creating a shared-custody plan or making one work.

A soft negotiator, by contrast, is someone who:
- Hates conflict or perhaps even fears it
- Tends to be trusting
- Wants to stay friends and work things out pleasantly
- Will give in if pushed hard enough
- Will disclose their bottom line

Soft negotiators often have grown up surrounded by dysfunction and as a result, experience a great deal of internal distress when faced with having to deal with a higher-conflict person, go to court, or deal with lawyers.

Who wins when a hard negotiator and a soft negotiator go up against each other in custody dispute? If you are like most parents, you are certain the answer is: the hard negotiator. The assumption people make is that the hard negotiator will steamroll the soft negotiator and win every time. If you think the correct answer is: the soft negotiator, it's likely because you believe the gentle heart always prevails in the end. If you are like the small minority (perhaps 2%) of the thousands of parents to whom I have put this question, you understand that neither wins. The truth is that no matter how effective these negotiating styles are in other settings, they only make things worse when a shared-custody dispute is on the table.

One reason both fail is that hard- and soft-negotiating approaches create weak contracts instead of strong agreements. The intimidating tactics used by a hard negotiator may initially be effective at getting the soft negotiator to "sign." At some point, however, the soft negotiator will begin feeling taken advantage of. Anger and resentment will build until the soft negotiator stops following the contract and hires a pit-bull attorney. Presto, without realizing it, the person playing hardball has transformed the soft negotiator into a hard negotiator. What happens when two angry hard negotiators go up against each other in a custody dispute? A train wreck.

Another reason why these negotiating approaches don't work is because they unnecessarily drag out the problem-solving process. Working out who is going to have the kids on Thanksgiving in odd years, what the pickup time will be on Sundays, and who will pay for the karate lessons doesn't need to involve elaborate maneuvering, continuances, and discovery testimony.

The bottom line is this: If you use a calmly assertive negotiating style with your ex, rather than "hard" or "soft" you will find that working out shared custody problems can be easy and painless. With that foundation in place, you are ready to learn four important rules for negotiating a lasting custody agreement.

FOUR RULES OF NEGOTIATION

In chapter two, I introduced principles that define a "win" in a custody dispute. They were that a "win" should: meet both parties' legitimate interests, improve the shared-custody relationship, involve an efficient and fair process, and produce a lasting agreement. According to Roger Fisher and William Ury in their book *Getting to Yes*, negotiating an agreement using these principles becomes easier if you also use their four rules for negotiating.

Rule one—*Zero in on the problem:* Too often parents focus on problems they have with each other rather than on how to resolve their shared-custody issues. This is how a disagreement over a parent being late for a pick-up can lead to a letter from a lawyer saying he/she is unfit to care for the kids. Focusing only on specific shared-custody problems is an effective tool, because it asks us to zero in on the issue in dispute and work through it efficiently. In doing this, it is important to avoid such things as: blaming, demanding, or trying to control the other party.

Rule two—*Focus on interests not positions:* I was once approached by a distraught father who told me that he was about to take his ex back to court but was worried it was going to get ugly again. The problem, he said, was that despite sharing custody equally, both parents wanted more time with their children. It was an issue in which, according to the father, there could only be one winner.

When I asked about the custody plan, he told me it was imposed by the judge and that it wasn't working well for either parent. Rather than see the parents return to court, I encouraged them to work with a private mediator to update their plan so it would work better for everyone involved. In the end, they retained equal custody and avoided court, because they learned through mediation how to avoid taking adversarial positions and to focus instead on meeting the legitimate interests of their children and each other.

This example gets to the essence of how interests and positions are different. Initially both parents shared the same position—they wanted more than 50 percent custody time with their kids. When the mediator helped them shift to focusing on their underlying interests, they were able to modify their existing plan to give both parents more quality time with the kids without changing from 50-50.

When working with interests rather than positions, it is important not to act in a way that threatens the fundamental interests of either parent. Negotiating a lasting agreement cannot be accomplished if one person is proposing ideas that threaten the other parent's physical or financial wellbeing.

Rule three—*Let the other side win too*: In a negotiation, once the interests of both parties are defined, the next step is to brainstorm solution options. When you do this, whether it is with a private mediator, a parent coordinator, or just you and your ex working things out on your own, try to make sure your ex's needs are met, as well as your own. Meeting the legitimate needs of both parents is the key to establishing a lasting agreement. Remember that while pushing to get everything you want may earn you a victory at the bargaining table, it may also turn your ex into a resentful hard-negotiator.

Rule four—*Use a fair standard*: From time to time, even after zeroing in on the problem, focusing on interests, and brainstorming creative solution options, parents may find themselves at an impasse. In such cases, appealing to a fair, objective, and impartial standard upon which to base a resolution is the most effective way to break through an impasse.

For example, if two people were negotiating the resale value of a diamond wedding ring, they might use an objective standard for determining its market value. One way to do that would be to visit three jewelry appraisers and have each of them evaluate it. The average value would then be considered the fair market value of the ring. In using this type of process, both sides appeal to a fair standard and thereby remove the possibility of one side later claiming they were taken advantage of.

Unfortunately, when it comes to the family law system there are no universally accepted fair standards for decision making. There is the "best interests of the child" standard. But what does this mean? As noted in the first chapter, the "best interests of the child" often has more to do with which parent has the most persuasive attorney than with fairness. Without a concrete definition that both parents can agree is fair, the "best interests of the child" standard can't help parents break through an impasse.

The solution to this problem is to reach beyond the courts generic "best interests" standard and to use the existing shared-custody literature to create a standard that you and your ex can agree is fair. The first step would be to define the "best interests of our child." There are several well-written and detailed definitions available on the internet or in print. In his 2006 book The *Truth about Children and Divorce,* Robert Emery offers a solid example termed, "The Children's Bill of Rights in Divorce." This principle-based standard can be used to guide your decision making.

Once you have a "best interest of *our child*" standard in place, you still may find that in certain circumstances, your standard isn't specific enough to help break through an impasse. This is where you need to do a little more homework.

Let's say that the issue in dispute is how to share custody of a fourteen-month-old child in a manner that is developmentally appropriate. Dad wants 50-50 custody where the child will spend one day with him and the next day with mom. The mother, who is still breastfeeding, supports the 50-50 idea but is concerned about the child bouncing from home to home every day.

The solution to this problem is to agree to use a research-based standard for how to do this, such as one set out in John Hartson and Brenda Payne's *Creating Effective Parenting Plans.* Published by the Family Law Division of the American Bar Association in 2006, this book provides detailed shared-custody plans for children from birth through to age 18 and includes summaries of what the leading researchers in the field think about special issues. If I were working with this family I would recommend they use the guidelines laid out in chapter 3: Infant to Three Years Old. Doing so would provide the parents with a fair, objective, and developmentally appropriate standard for breaking through their impasse.

The book also provides similar objective guidelines for how co-parents can work with each other (Fifteen rules for Co-parenting, pg. 199, *Creating Effective Parenting Plans*) and for how to choose a doctor, therapist, or school. The key thing is to find a standard that is established in the literature, that is objective and fair.

Using the Four Rules of Negotiation effectively will take practice. If you are in a custody dispute with a hard negotiator or a high-conflict person, some additional reading will help you prepare yourself. Roger Fisher and Daniel Shapiro, in their book, *Beyond Reason: Using Emotions as You Negotiate*, offer practical strategies for negotiating with highly emotional people who tend to play by their own rules. In, *The Power of a Positive No: Save The Deal, Save The Relationship, and Still Say No*, William Ury, teaches the art of assertively saying no in a way that strengthens relationships. The book presents an intuitively simple framework for preparing for and successfully resolving any dispute.

Power Strategy #6—Building a Winning Team

Struggling through a difficult custody battle can be a long, lonely and exhausting journey. The stress can be overwhelming, causing extreme anxiety, anger, fear, sadness, and even despair. One of the best ways to turn things around and start them moving in the right direction is to build a winning team. Building a team dedicated to helping you achieve peaceful shared custody is essential. The following steps and criteria will help you build that team.

Purpose of the team: The first step is to decide what kind of a team you need. Do you need a team that provides mostly emotional support? Or one that offers emotional and strong legal support? Your answer will have a lot to do with the level of conflict in your case. If you are in a low-conflict situation, you may only need emotional support. If you are in a higher-conflict case, you should assemble a team that includes both emotional and legal support.

Vision and leadership: All successful teams have a vision of what they are trying to realize or achieve. Before building your team it is important for you to write out in detail what your goals are.

Successful teams also have assertive leaders. In order to develop a team that will help you arrive at peaceful shared custody, it is essential that you assume full responsibility for leading your team toward a principled resolution of your dispute. While being an assertive leader may seem intimidating, the truth is you already are in charge, whether you want the role or not. Regardless of what your mom, your friend, or your lawyer recommends, it is still you making the final decisions. The real question you need to answer is this: am I going to blame everyone else for the fact that my custody dispute is a mess, or am I going to take full responsibility for the mess and assemble a team to clean it up?

Positive vs. negative team members: It is important that you choose people who are going to work with you, not against you. For example, if your attorney, therapist, mother, or new partner is constantly pushing you to steamroll your ex, you may want to consider looking elsewhere for advice. Cynical, self-righteous, and greedy people tend to make poor team players. This is because they undermine the kind of positive, hopeful, and forward-thinking energy that successful teams thrive on. Choose your team members carefully.

Assemble a team: Now, with a vision of the right team in mind, assemble that team. If you have in mind a team that will help you cope with the emotional side-effects of your situation, you may be leaning toward an informal group of family or friends who have agreed to advise and support you. If the issues are of a more complicated nature, you may be contemplating finding a therapist or a shared-custody coach. If you are in a moderate- or high-conflict dispute, you should be thinking of adding ADR-focused legal, mental health, financial, and other professionals, as suit your needs.

Put your team to work: Once your support team is in place, it's time to get to work. At this stage, it is very important for you to have realistic expectations and stay focused on laying a solid foundation for the future.

Assess and adapt: Custody battles have a way of taking unexpected twists and turns. It is therefore important that you keep monitoring the effectiveness of your team as the dispute progresses. At some point, you may find a need to bring in someone new or let someone go.

Finally, it is important to keep in mind that depending on how complicated the issues are in your case, positive results may take time to emerge. If you begin to doubt the wisdom of approaching your dispute in this "high road" way, remind yourself to trust the process. Also, remember that your kids are watching. Every time you make a peaceful step you are role modeling for them how to handle difficult life problems in a way that places integrity and respect above bitterness and deceit. These are the kinds of priceless lessons your children need to learn from you, especially if your ex is on a different path.

Power Strategy #7—Break Out of the Stress Hurricane

A mother who was going through a grueling custody battle once told me that she felt like she was stuck in a "stress hurricane." She was not sure if she would survive. Feeling this way is not uncommon. In fact, fighting over custody may be the most stressful situation you will face in your lifetime. It doesn't matter if you are a parent, step-parent, grandparent, or one of the children involved, no one escapes the nerve-wracking reach of a battle over custody.

According to university researchers, the two most stressful things in life are the death of a spouse and going through separation or divorce. Just behind these are: a close family member going to jail, a serious illness, getting fired, moving, and going broke. Notable is the fact that one or more of these circumstances often arise in a custody dispute.

Now you might be saying, "I'm going through a really difficult custody fight, but I'm fine. I feel a little stressed sometimes ,but it's not too bad." This is very common. But it's difficult to gauge our own level of stress. Typically, we need a neutral third person, like a mental health professional, to accurately assess stress. There are also written tests that can determine levels of stress and how well we respond to that stress. Interestingly, even once they learn how stressed they are, parents in a custody dispute often do a poor job of getting it under control. This, in large part, is because of common misconceptions about stress and how to manage it.

Many people think that the way to reduce stress is to eliminate the stressors behind it. This is logical thinking. If x stresses me out, avoid x. I can only imagine what the mother who told me she was living inside a "stress hurricane" would have said if I told her, "The trick is to avoid the things that are stressing you out." To do that she would have had to avoid going to work, going home, dealing with her sick mother, and each one of her kids. The truth is that most of the stressors in our world are beyond our control. We can't just say, "It stresses me out when the baby cries, so I will avoid the baby."

What I *did* tell the mother was to figure out where she fit on the stress-personality scale, and then start learning and implementing the strategies needed to move toward a low-stress life. Let me explain this concept using two characters from the popular Disney movie, *Finding Nemo*.

Marlin, Nemo's dad, is a stressed-out fish. I think we would all agree that he has every right to be. As the film opens, his home is invaded and his wife and all but one of his children are eaten. As a single father raising a disabled fish—if you recall, Nemo has a bad fin—Marlin seems to be overwhelmed at every turn. He worries about his son starting school, getting picked on, and going too close to the drop-off. If it wasn't for Nemo's tenacious spirit, I think Marlin would be content to see the two of them never leave the protection of the anemone. I think you would agree, if Marlin took the stress-personality test, he'd likely be off the scale.

Crush, on the other hand, is very different. A calm and laid-back turtle, he is the kind of parent we would like for ourselves. At one point in the film, Crush's son falls out of the EAC (East Australian Current). Does Crush have a meltdown or call 911? No. Moments later, when the little one swims back into the EAC, his dad beams proudly and cries out, "Rrrrrrighteous." We all know someone like Crush, someone who doesn't let things get to him or her. Even big things like divorce are easier to manage when you are more like Crush than Marlin.

Now let's imagine that Marlin and Crush are swimming down the worst street in your neighborhood at midnight when all of a sudden they see a homeless fish coming towards them. As the fish gets closer, what do you think is going through Marlin's mind? I imagine he would be saying to himself. "This fish looks like trouble. I bet he has a gun or a knife. If he killed me, who will take care of Nemo? Who will keep him away from the drop-off? Crush, on the other hand, would likely be thinking something very different, such as, "Boy, this guy sure looks down on his luck. I wish I had a couple bucks to help him out. Times sure are tough." When the homeless fish passes without incident, Marlin would be thinking, "Phew, that was close. That crazy guy was dangerous with a capital D. I hope he isn't a stalker, maybe we should run." While Crush would likely say to himself, "Poor guy. I know he'll bounce back."

This scenario illustrates the essential link between our stress level and the way we perceive the stressors in our world. While Marlin and Crush were in the same situation—in an alley with a homeless fish—one perceived threat while the other felt compassion. A scan of Crush's brain would show a mind that is in balance and serene. On the other hand, Marlin's brain scan would reveal a tormented mind firing and misfiring on all cylinders. This is because the two interpret sensory input very differently. Marlin sees danger everywhere, while Crush doesn't. Who do you think is the happier of the two?

We all need to learn to be less like Marlin and more like Crush. I will explain how this can be done, but first I'd like to address a bigger problem: the common misconception by parents in a custody dispute that they either don't have a high-stress personality or that they "have it under control."

At this point I'd like you to take my, "Are You a Marlin or a Crush?" test to determine your general level of stress. Which of the two do you think you are more like? Let's find out.

Are you a Marlin or a Crush?
Using a scale of 1 to 5 – with 1 being I don't think this way and 5 being I always think this way, please answer the following questions:

1.   Slow drivers make me nuts. __
2.   I set high expectation for myself and others. __
3.   I would rather watch a good movie than go exercise. __
4.   I am competitive; I hate to lose. __
5.   I feel guilty often. __
6.   I prefer to be in control of things rather than to delegate. __
7.   Saying "no" can be hard for me. __
8.   I try and avoid conflict. __
9.   Unfairness bugs me. __
10. I hate waiting for things. __
11. I like things to be my version of perfect. __
12. I get so frustrated I feel like I'm going to explode. __
13. I rarely feel rested. __
14. I wish people were better listeners. __
15. I can always think of a reason to put things off. __

Your Score___/75

Scoring
This test is designed to highlight how your perception of the world shapes your life experiences. Rather than asking about specific stressors that can be avoided, it focuses on the beliefs and expectations that shape how you react to stressors that can't be avoided. Take for example Question # 10, "I hate waiting for things." I think we can all imagine what it might look like if Marlin and Crush went together to a doctor's appointment and had to wait for an hour. Crush would be

sound asleep and Marlin would be pacing and muttering about how put out he is.

Less than 25
You are a lot like Crush, easy-going, the kind of person who rarely gets worked up. You enjoy life moment by moment and can't see why so many people have so much drama in their lives. You would always choose a margarita at sunset over staying late at the office, and would rather watch a good movie with a loved one than make sure the cans in the pantry are lined up right.

26-39
You're stress level is on par with Crush's edgy cousin. Your beliefs and attitude make you susceptible to mild to moderate stress levels. You are healthy and balanced, but are prone to talking yourself into feeling anxious about little things. While you have a tendency to avoid conflict and to procrastinate, you are a happy person, for the most part.

40-54
You resemble Marlin's calm twin. Your thoughts about the world around you cause you to regularly experience moderate to high levels of stress. You are frequently frustrated by the fact that the people around you don't listen to you or take your advice. You don't like confrontations but the perfectionist side of you gets upset easily. Rather than dealing with things assertively, you avoid and let them slowly build until one day you explode over something small.

55+
You are just like Marlin. If you look deep within, you will see that you are anxious and unhappy most of the time. For the most part you are dissatisfied with yourself, those around you, and the circumstances of your life. You have a hard time staying in healthy relationships, have a tendency to use or abuse substances to help you stay calm, and

have been encouraged at least once to get some help for anxiety or depression.

If you are like most of the people I give this test to, you've just learned something important about yourself. Despite believing all your life that you were a relatively calm person, you now see that your general stress level is higher than you thought. Some of you probably doubt the accuracy of the test, especially those scoring 55+. So let's take a look at what the research tells us about how high-stress personalities are formed and see if it sounds familiar.

As parents, we all know that children are born with different temperaments. Some kids can sleep through an earthquake and others get anxious over the smallest things. While there is clearly some genetic component at play, it appears that personality is more a product of environment. Not surprisingly, a child raised in a high-stress environment is likely to develop high-stress personality traits.

While kids won't usually describe their home life as highly stressful—because it's the only environment they have ever known—when we look back as adults on our own childhoods, we are often able to see things more clearly. Looking back, how many of these things had an impact on your upbringing?

- Substance abuse: Did your parent, step parent or some other person(s) you were close to use or abuse substances?
- Fear: Were you raised by people who would use violence to intimidate and control you or others at home?
- Expectations: Were you ever good enough? Was it difficult living up to the expectations others set for you?
- Negativity: Was there a lot of thinking, talking and focusing on the negative side of things?
- Over-reacting: Were your parents more likely to avoid or over-react to stressful situations? Were you able to predict how they would react?

- Anxiousness: Were one or both of your parents nervous, anxious, or unsure of themselves when outside of their normal setting or routine?
- Panic: Did either of your parents struggle with post traumatic stress, anxiety attacks, or social anxiety?
- Grief and loss: Were their significant broken attachments with key people in your life due to divorce, death, imprisonment, or some other reason?

Now that you have looked at whether or not you grew up in a high-stress environment, the next thing you need to do is ask yourself whether you are raising your children in a similar environment. Perhaps they were raised in such an environment while your stressed-out ex was still in the home. Either way, it is important that you answer honestly, even though it may be difficult to remain objective.

When a child grows up in a high stress environment, certain personality traits develop. Look at the list of traits below. Do you recognize these traits in yourself or in your kids?

- Defensiveness—overly sensitive to criticism
- A tendency to avoid or overreact
- Low self-esteem
- Fierce competitiveness—hate to lose
- Feel guilty often
- Anxious or nervous
- Indecisiveness—difficulty making decisions
- Easily embarrassed
- An analytical and obsessive thinker
- Perfectionism
- Very concerned with what others think
- A catastrophic thinker—often worries something really bad will happen
- The tendency to worry about many things simultaneously
- Need to be (or at the very least appear to be) in control

117

Do these traits look familiar? Can you see some of them in yourself or your ex? How about your kids? According to the research, children who grow up with high-stress parents are seven times more likely to develop a stress disorder.

Higher-stress people tend to overreact internally, in response to what they perceive externally. The way Marlin responded to the homeless fish is a good example. If you were to follow Marlin around all day for a week, you would find that he hits his internal panic button multiple times per day, every day. As you might imagine, Marlin is always worried that something bad is about to happen.

After a while, the Marlins of the world get worn out and begin to feel depressed (according to research, about 75 percent of high-stress people struggle with low energy, fatigue, and exhaustion). Think of it as being on a high-stress merry-go-round. Those like Marlin, eventually get worn out and have trouble keeping up with their daily routine. On and on it goes, day in and day out.

Of course not everyone with a high-stress personality is exactly like Marlin. Here is a list of symptoms experienced by people with high stress. Some may only experience two or three, but others will recognize them all.

- Racing heart
- Shortness of breath
- Trembling
- Nausea
- Aches and pains
- Fatigue
- Dizziness
- Headaches
- Difficulty getting to sleep or staying asleep
- Muscle tension
- Feelings of unreality
- Scary or uncontrollable thoughts

- Fear of going crazy, hurting yourself or someone else
- Depressed feelings
- Exhaustion
- Panic
- Not wanting to drive, leave the house, or get on a plane

Now that you can identify markers that indicate a high-stress personality, and how such a personality develops, the key to reducing your stress level is to change the way you think. Here is how to become more like Crush in three easy steps.

Step One—Look in the mirror
Before anyone can turn the tables on high stress, they have to be willing to admit they have a higher-stress personality. This is not easy; it is difficult to be objective when it comes to looking at ourselves. Let's go back to Marlin for a moment. If you were to ask him whether he thinks he is a high stress fish, he would probably say no and defensively explain, in much detail, why he has good reasons to be worried all the time. Then he would swim back to his anemone and replay the conversation over and over in his head, coming up with things he wished he had said. This would go on until a new concern came along to take its place.

While you may be reluctant to admit you have a higher-stress personality, I am not asking you to disclose it on *Oprah*; just to admit it to yourself. You see, the purpose of this section of the book is not to embarrass you, but to help you better know yourself so you can deal with the overwhelming stress of a custody battle. It is also intended to help you better understand what your ex may be coping with, and to deepen your understanding of what your kids may be experiencing.

Step Two—Complete a stress-reduction program
Stress-reduction programs frequently cost almost nothing, are usually completed at home, and are highly effective. Let me tell you briefly about three programs I like to recommend to my clients.

119

The first was developed by Jon Kabat-Zinn and launched at the University of Massachusetts Medical Center in 1979. Referred to as Mindfulness-Based Stress Reduction (MBSR), this program is used in hospitals, clinics, and counseling offices worldwide. It helps people learn how to use their "innate resources and abilities to respond more effectively to stress, pain, and illness." More than 17,000 people have completed the eight-week program.

The program's effectiveness has been rigorously proven in the lab and in treatment, and it is affordable. For people who would like to complete the program with a mental health professional, the MBSR Web site at the University of Massachusetts maintains a directory of people who are MBSR certified.

Those who prefer to save a few bucks by completing the program at home can find it in Kabat-Zinn's *Full Catastrophe Living: Using the Wisdom of Your Body and Mind to Face Stress, Pain and Illness.* I suggest you also purchase the companion CD set of stress-reduction materials called *Mindfulness Meditation*, sets 1 and 2, as well as Kabat-Zinn's book *Wherever you Go, There you Are.* You should be able to pick up all these materials for under $50, if you look for them used online.

Another effective program is one designed for adults who are struggling with panic attacks, agoraphobia (typically experienced as a fear of leaving the house), or anxiety attacks. Developed by David Barlow and Michelle Craske, *Mastery of Your Anxiety and Panic* is an evidence-based treatment designed to eliminate the panic, agoraphobia, and anxiety attacks that are so paralyzing for so many. Offered in workbook format, this program is simple to use, very effective, and can be purchased for under $25.

The third program is one designed for kids and teens. *The Life Skills Program*, developed by CHAANGE Anxiety and Treatment Programs, is a structured program that teaches school-aged children and teens how to cope more effectively with fear and anxiety. Designed so that parents can guide their children through the process without having to pay for expensive counseling, this program teaches young people how to change the way they think. Topics include relaxation, self-esteem, assertiveness, and living fearlessly, to name a few.

Step 3—Take care of yourself

Our ability to get and stay in balance has a lot to with how well we eat, exercise, and sleep. Walking from the fridge to the den and falling asleep in front of the TV after reheating yesterday's pizza is the opposite of what I am talking about. The stress of a child custody marathon drains us in profound ways. One of the key ways is through exhaustion, which is brought on when we neglect to give ourselves the fuel needed for such a long race.

If this is an area where you could use some assistance, there are two books you may want to consider reading. The first is by Deepak Chopra. In, *Perfect Health: The Complete Mind/Body Guide*, and in the workshop by the same name, Dr. Chopra explains that health is not merely the absence of disease. In order to live a full and vital life one must understand the connection between wellness, balance, and physical health. This book offers a practical road map for how to do just that.

In, *8 Weeks to Optimum Health: A Proven Program for Taking Full Advantage of Your Body's Natural Healing Power*, Dr. Andrew Weil, offers a structured step-by-step approach to improving health. Built on the concept that health and healing are intrinsically linked, this book guides readers on a holistic journey toward, strength, vitality, and inner balance.

SECTION THREE:

Making it Work in the Real World

Five Simple Steps

When confronted with a big or a small shared custody problem, use the following *Five Simple Steps:*

Step One—What are the core problems?
This first step may be the most important, because if you can't figure what the core problems are, how can you possibly develop a plan for fixing them? In order to determine the central issues, ask yourself, and possibly the people on your team:

- What are the specific problems in our dispute (e.g. a high-conflict ex, money, fear, parenting disagreements, etc.).
- What problems are being made worse by the battle (e.g. cost of going to court, child doing poorly in school, etc.)?
- Am I in some way part of the problem (e.g. having unrealistic expectations, a too hard or soft bargaining posture, by not managing the stress well, or in some other way)?
- Are our child struggling in a way that could be considered a core problem (e.g. struggling in school, getting into fights or acting depressed)?

Step Two—What are the options?
Once you have a good sense of the core problems, it's time to dig into the research literature and see what the experts say is the most effective way to resolve the problems. While your situation may feel unique, remember that divorced and separated parents all over the world struggle with the same problems, and there are effective ways of

125

dealing with them. With research in hand, it's time to begin mapping out a strategy. Depending on the issue, you may choose to do this on your own or in consultation with your emotional or legal team members.

Step Three—Get prepared to negotiate

Having decided on a plan of action, you now need to get prepared. Be careful: rushing or skipping this stage is a big mistake. It is critical that you take the time to think through scenarios of how things may play out, and prepare yourself for possible eventualities.

Step Four—Work it out

Whether you hope to work out your problem with your ex over coffee at Starbucks, use private mediation, a collaborative team, or do it through a parent coordinator, it is important that you launch your plan with confidence and from a position of power.

Step Five—Keep working at it

Turning a difficult custody situation around is not something that will happen in a day, a week, or a month. You will make mistakes. Be open about it when you do. Your ex will make mistakes also. Try and be forgiving. It can feel as if you are taking two steps forward and three steps back at times. A well-functioning co-parenting relationship takes time to build. Be patient and remember that you are doing all of this for your kids.

Gracie's New School
—A Low-Conflict Case

Ron and Abbey had been together eleven months when Gracie was born. At the time they had busy careers and didn't want to be parents, at least not until they were in their thirties and were confident their relationship was going to last. But for the baby's sake they crossed their fingers and got married. The next day, Gracie was born.

For two years they tried to make it work. But the fatigue associated with parenting a newborn, pressures at work, and very different views on how to parent slowly took their toll. It was Abbey who first suggested divorce, but they both knew things were not working. They were too different.

Ron and Abbey chose to work out the terms of their divorce and develop a shared-custody plan with a private mediator. They chose a family law attorney to serve as the mediator and worked out a fair settlement in four sessions. In the end, they agreed to share custody equally. Gracie would spend one week at her dad's and the next at her mom's.

While Abbey and Ron had small problems from time to time, things went well until Gracie started second grade. According to her new teacher, Gracie was fidgeting too much, blurting out answers without putting her hand up, was overly talkative, and not handing in her homework. The teacher recommended an evaluation to see if Gracie had attention-deficit hyperactivity (ADHD) disorder. Gracie's pediatrician diagnosed her with ADHD and gave the parents a prescription for Ritalin. Then things got messy.

Abbey was completely against using medication. Instead of putting Gracie on Ritalin, she proposed, they should send her to a private school that had small classrooms and more support. It would also cost both parents $400 a month. Ron, on the other hand, had been on Ritalin from age nine to fourteen and felt his daughter would benefit. He liked the public school she was attending and wanted her to stay there.

When it became clear that they were stuck, they called the private mediator who had helped them settle their divorce. At the end of their brief three-way call, the mediator e-mailed them the New Way to Win *five simple steps* process for working through their problem and suggested they make an appointment to meet in one week, if they couldn't work things out on their own.

Both parents completed steps one to three and then met at Starbucks. Ron explained that he felt the core problem (dealt with in step one) was Gracie's ADHD and her mother's reluctance to use medication to treat it. Abbey agreed and added that, private school at $800 a month would be difficult to manage, though she still thought it was the best way to go.

According to Abbey's research (step two), medication was only one way to address attention problems. The alternatives, she explained, focused on maintaining a healthy diet, getting plenty of sleep, lots of exercise, and teaching the child organization, focus, and social skills. Ron, still not convinced, presented Abbey with a document showing that ADHD medications are safe.

Before their meeting at Starbucks, both Ron and Abbey had thought through how their conversation might go (step three—get prepared) and were ready to propose ideas for resolving their impasse. Ron started (step four—work it out) by suggesting Gracie stay in her current school and start on the medication. At the same time both parents would make sure her diet, sleep, and exercise needs were met. In addition, Gracie would begin an organization, focus and social skills program called *Skillstreaming the Elementary School Child*. If in three months the situation did not improve, Ron would look for a second job to earn the money needed to move Gracie to the private school.

Abbey's counter proposal was to leave Gracie in public school and to have her complete a standardized test for ADHD right away and then again in three months. During that interim she would not be on medication. Instead, the focus would be on sleep, exercise, healthy eating, and teaching Gracie organization, focus, and social skills. After three months, if the standardized testing didn't show improvement, she would agree to try Gracie on the medication for the final three months of the year. If by the end of grade two Gracie was still struggling, she would be transferred to the private school the following year.

The parents left Starbucks with a fair agreement that was later written up by Ron and e-mailed to Abbey and their private mediator. Over the weeks and months that followed, Gracie did better, thanks to the effort made by both parents to earnestly put into action their agreement (step five—make it work).

"You are always late" —A Moderate Conflict Case

Karen's new husband, Randy, was an accountant and a stickler for details. One of his pet peeves was waiting. He hated it when meetings didn't start on time. In this respect he was the exact opposite of Karen's first husband Grayson, who was never on time for anything in his life.

Karen's relationship with Grayson had always been turbulent. Grayson was a drummer who still played with a band in the Los Angeles club scene. He worked late, partied hard, and flew off the handle when he didn't get what he wanted. He had always enjoyed making new female friends whenever possible. Karen and Grayson had done pretty well sharing custody of their twin boys since she left him nine years ago. At least, that is, until Randy came on the scene.

Shortly after getting married, Randy started driving the boys to Grayson's apartment when it was his time to have them. After several weeks in a row where Randy waited more than thirty minutes for Grayson to show up, Randy blew up at Karen, saying he would no longer drive the kids to their dad's house.

Karen contacted her ex and asked him to begin picking the kids up at her house, and said that she would pick them up at his house when it was time for them to come home. That didn't work either because Dad never made it back from Disneyland or some other exciting Sunday adventure on time for the scheduled pick-up. Even though Randy did not participate in the pick-ups, it still bugged him that Grayson was always late. And it didn't help matters when the boys told him that Grayson had started calling him "Mr. Bean."

One night, things turned ugly. Randy was telling Grayson that he was setting a poor example by being late all the time, when Grayson asked him if he wanted to settle things outside. Randy demanded Grayson leave the house, but he refused. When Randy picked up the phone and said he was calling the police, Grayson took off. The next day, there were two long scratches along the full length of Randy's new car.

A week later Karen received a letter from an attorney stating that Randy was behaving in a hostile manner that interfered with Grayson's relationship with the twins. It went on to suggest that Randy seek counseling and that if his "grossly inappropriate behavior" continued, the attorney would ask the court to grant a restraining order. The next day, Karen and Randy paid a six-thousand dollar retainer to hire a local attorney they found in the yellow pages.

Over the next two years, things got worse. Lawyer letters went back and forth and court dates followed. No issue was too small to go unchallenged. The tension got so heavy that the boys started dreading pick-ups and drop-offs, which never took place without a lot of arguing and yelling.

Things began to change, however, when the judge denied Karen's request that Grayson undergo a psychiatric evaluation and instead ordered both parents to attend a higher-conflict co-parenting education program. According to the judge, both parents needed to learn the skills required to more effectively share custody of their boys. Neither parent had heard of such a program, and both resented the implication that they needed to attend a parenting class.

During the ten-hour class, they were introduced to many of the concepts presented in this book. They were also encouraged to make an appointment with a private child custody mediator who specializes in higher-conflict disputes and use the Five Simple Steps found in this book to prepare for the first session.

Prior to the first session, Karen sat down with Randy and went through the steps. Together they identified the following core problems (step one): mistrust, poor communication, Randy's controlling nature, Grayson's higher-conflict personality, Karen's tendency toward being passive and anxious, the expense of having lawyers involved, and the fact that the kids were showing signs of depression and increased aggression. Grayson made his own list that included: Randy's quarrelsome ways, the fact that he had spent $21,000 dollars on lawyer fees, and his concern that his parenting time might be reduced by the judge.

In exploring his options (step two) Grayson read the book Mom's House Dad's House and did some research online at www. PeacefulSharedCustody.com. He decided he would take a more business-like approach to working with Karen and "Mr. Bean," which included being on time for the kids' sake, doing curbside drop offs so that he didn't have to see or speak with Randy, and using a log book to communicate about parenting matters rather than talking on the phone.

Karen also did research online and bought a couple of books. Her list of options focused on the importance of getting the kids into counseling, how to work effectively with a higher-conflict personality, and how she could better manage stress and become more assertive.

By the time Grayson and Karen sat down with their private child custody mediator, they were ready to begin a productive negotiation. While it looked as if the mediation process would break down when Grayson stormed out of the second meeting, by the end of the seventh session the parents had worked things out. At the mediator's urging, the children met with her before the fourth session to share their concerns and perspective. Even Randy participated, by attending the final "full family" session, where he pledged his support for the new plan.

A key element of their settlement involved looking at how they would make their agreement work in the real world (step five). With this in mind, they developed a problem-solving protocol designed to prevent minor shared-custody problems from escalating to the point of involving lawyers. Should a problem arise, the parents agreed to send an e-mail explaining the problem and proposing one or more solutions. If after going back and forth using e-mail, the problem was not resolved, the parents would forward their e-mails to their private mediator and do a three-way call in an attempt to resolve the problem. If the call was unsuccessful, the parents would meet with their private mediator for a formal session. The parents agreed to involve their lawyers only if all of these processes were exhausted.

Finally, the private mediator also suggested that both parents consider working with their own co-parenting coach. She explained that the coach would be available by phone when a problem came up and would help brainstorm effective ways to resolve the situation. The mediator encouraged the parents to go to the Professionals Directory on www.PeacefulSharedCustody.com and find a coach with expertise in child custody, high conflict, and mediation. The coach, she added, would bring a strong and constructive voice to each parent's team, and if ever needed, could write a letter to the court detailing the effort made by the client to proactively work through shared custody problems.

"Stop brainwashing Sarah" —A High Conflict Case

Martin and Jane were drinking buddies at first. Then they got into drugs. Martin eventually cleaned himself up and even joined the police force, but Jane never really got off the drugs. She managed to quit cocaine after ordered by the court to enter drug treatment, but then she got hooked on the prescription drugs the doctor gave her for sleep, pain, and anxiety.

From age fourteen, Jane had been in and out of counseling and had even had two short stays in a psychiatric hospital after talking about wanting to kill herself. Jane hated to be alone, felt empty inside much of the time, and felt that people were always abandoning her.

While Martin was able to conquer his addiction to drugs, he never learned to control his jealousy or anger. Several times during his on-and-off-again relationship with Jane, he had nearly been arrested for spousal assault. Once, after accusing Jane of fooling around, he pushed her into a book shelf. She was cut badly and nearly lost the use of her left eye. Martin, of course, was immediately remorseful, and Jane agreed not to call the police.

Martin and Jane's daughter, Sarah, was born during their bad drug period. Thankfully, Sarah doesn't remember those times. She was only three when her parents broke up. Though her dad seemed to care, he often failed to visit when he was supposed to and made promises he didn't keep. When Sarah finally got mad and refused to see him,

135

Martin left Jane a phone message threatening to take her back to court if she didn't stop the brainwashing.

Jane felt that her life was starting to improve after she took out a restraining order against Martin and found a job working as a substance abuse counselor. Martin's life was as also getting better. He had a new girlfriend and more money, having been promoted to detective.

Unfortunately, all this didn't change the fact that Jane and Martin had been fighting over custody, child support, and parenting issues for most of Sarah's life. They had been to court on thirty-six occasions in six years, and Martin had fired five lawyers. Even though he was fed up with lawyers, he couldn't have hired a sixth even had he wanted to. His raise in pay was insufficient to cover his mounting legal bills. Jane's legal fees, fortunately for her, were covered by her parents.

Martin and Jane had completed a court ordered, high-conflict co-parenting class and Martin did a sixteen-week anger-management program. Private mediation was attempted, but because Martin was unable to control his anger, the mediator discontinued the process and referred the case back to court. Two child-custody evaluations were conducted, the second after Martin's lawyer persuaded the judge that the first evaluator showed a bias towards Jane. After six years of wrangling and court-ordered programs, Martin had spent $78,000 and Jane $33,000.

At their most recent court hearing, the judge modified the restraining order to allow for shared-parenting communication and ordered a parent coordinator be assigned to the case for two years. The parenting coordinator started his work by meeting with both parents separately and then with Sarah. He introduced Martin and Jane to a structured five-step process for working through all future shared custody disputes.

It was agreed that all communications between them would be in writing and stored in the online log book at OurFamilyWizard.com, a web-based resource designed to facilitate high-conflict, shared-custody situations. For the first six months, the parent coordinator monitored all communications between the parents. He also met with Sarah once a month to make sure she was doing well, and ordered both parents to start counseling.

Martin responded positively to the parent coordinator. Having someone other than an indifferent lawyer to call when a problem arose suited him well. He liked the structured process he had been given for working through disputes and appreciated that Jane was using the same approach. Perhaps what he liked most was the fact that the parent coordinator had the power to make decisions and then file them with the court, keeping him out of court for the last year.

Jane, too, was pleased with the parent coordinator. Having someone who knew the case inside out and who knew Sarah, made a big difference. Jane felt that the coordinator had helped both parents to recognize the importance of thinking problems through before responding. Not doing so in the past, she realized, had been self-sabotaging.

Nine-year-old Sarah felt that she finally had someone who listened to her. She appreciated how the parent coordinator encouraged her to be fair but firm with her parents. She liked meeting with him for the first six months. Now she only talks with him by phone if something comes up. She is proud of the progress her parents have made, and enjoys her time with them more than ever.

Conclusion

You are powerful. You are a leader. You can protect your children and resolve your custody dispute. You can do it by committing yourself to winning—a new way. Please keep in mind, however, that winning is a journey not a destination. There will be times when you will doubt the wisdom of choosing the "high road." When this happens, take out a picture of your children, or grandchildren, and whisper these words, "I am doing this for you. I love you."

Whether you are a parent, step parent, or a grandparent, remind yourself that every time you make a peaceful step, you are teaching the children how to do the same thing. You are showing them how powerful they can be. That, like you, they have the ability to change their world for the better.

In the movie, *Pay it Forward*, Kevin Spacey plays Eugene Simonet, a social studies teacher who challenges his seventh grade students to "take the things you don't like about this world and flip them upside down." Their homework assignment, Spacey explains, is to come up with a way to change the world, and then put it into action.

In response, student Trevor McKinney creates a plan to "pay it forward." He will do a favor or good deed for three people, and rather than looking for some kind of payback, he will ask each of the three to "pay it forward" by doing a good deed for three other people.

Presenting his plan to the class, Trevor says "I am going to help three people. But it has to be something really big. Something they can't do for themselves. So I will do it for them. Then they will do it for three other people—that's nine. And they will do it for three other people. Then it starts to get big really fast."

Take the skills, ideas, and strategies in this book and do something really big for your kids. Change their world, and yours, by finding a new to win your custody dispute. Then pay it forward by sharing your success story and wisdom with parents around the world at, www. PeacefulSharedCustody.com, or by sending your copy of this book to someone who needs it with a "pay it forward" note.

Appendix

Helping our Adult Children:
A Framework for Grandparents

Grandparents struggle in profound ways when their children separate or divorce. In addition to working through their own feelings of loss related to the breakdown of their child's family, grandparents often face a range of difficult choices. How involved should I get? Should I take sides? Should I pay for my child's lawyer? Should I get a lawyer? What if my child wants to move in with me? How do I help my grandchildren adjust? How do I promote a peaceful resolution to all of this?

As with all custody disputes the stakes are high. Too often grandparents find themselves cut off from their grandchildren with little they can do to remedy the situation. In other cases, grandparents are asked to come out of retirement and assume a full-time child-care provider role. Still others are asked to tap into their savings to pay the legal fees associated with an ugly custody battle. What are grandparents to do?

The following ten strategies are designed to provide you with a framework for helping your children, grandchildren, and yourself. Whether you are trying to help your child avoid a custody battle in the first place, or your goal is to help untangle an ongoing custody mess, these strategies will show you how to encourage a quick and peaceful end to the fighting.

1. *Do your Homework*: Before involving yourself in your child's separation or divorce, it is essential that you educate yourself as to the options available in your area for peacefully resolving child-custody problems. You can find out how your local

family law court works by looking it up online or by going to the courthouse and asking your questions to a court facilitator. Make sure to familiarize yourself with how a family law case proceeds through the court system. For example, will the parents have to complete a co-parenting education program? Will they be required to attend court-based mediation? What are the grandparent visitation laws in your area? Is there a local legal-aid clinic where your child could get free legal assistance? You should also ask for a list of local counselors, programs, visitation monitors, and support groups for divorced and separated families.

In addition to learning about the local court process, it is important that you familiarize yourself with the options available to parents for resolving their custody dispute peacefully. This book sketches out a road map for how to do just that. For additional information, or to ask other grandparents for advice, go to www.PeacefulSharedCustody. com.

2. *Visualize a role for yourself:* Think carefully about the role you want to play before you get involved. How can you serve as a peacemaker? In what ways can you help your grandchildren? How are you going to respond to requests for money for legal fees or other things? Do you have the assertiveness skills needed to set healthy boundaries with your child? Do you have support people in your life that you can talk to about this situation when you need to? When your grandchildren look back on this period in their lives, what would you like them to remember about the role you played in helping them through it?

3. *Stay Neutral:* Avoid taking sides even if you come to learn troubling information about one or both parents. Instead,

reach out to both parents and encourage them to find ways to peacefully resolve their dispute. Let them know that your highest priority is to help your grandkids through this difficult time. Ask for their ideas on how you can do this. Avoid getting directly involved with the legal issues. Resist writing a letter to the court for either parent.

If you have already taken sides—you may want to rethink your approach. Consider switching to a neutral posture, while at the same time encouraging both parents to work things out peacefully. When the custody matter is finally resolved, this will help ensure that you continue to have stable and consistent contact with your grandchildren.

4. *Encourage both parents to protect their children*: Many parents are unaware of how harmful a custody dispute can be on kids. Encourage both parents to learn about this issue either by going online, purchasing a book, or attending a co-parenting education class.

   If the dispute has been going on for some time and one or more of your grandchildren appear to be suffering, encourage the parents to consider starting the child in counseling. Keep in mind, however, that it is very important to find a counselor who specializes in this area. You can get a list of questions to ask a prospective counselor on www.ANewWaytoWin.com.

5. *Help both parents learn about their resolution options*: Many parents are not aware of the highly-effective (and cost-efficient) options available to them. Encourage both parents to learn about these options and to earnestly use them to try and resolve their dispute. Be prepared for one or both parents to tell you "I've already tried that," or "It will never work—you don't understand how irrational the other parent is," or

"I don't have time for all that—my lawyer has things under control." A good response might be to say, "You may be right, but I would hate to see you spend thousands of dollars on a custody battle and end up worse off. How could it hurt to explore your other options?"

6. *Use your limited funds wisely—resist lending large sums of money*: If your child is out of work, or is otherwise in need of financial support, it is likely that you will be asked to help out. Think this issue through carefully before you commit to anything. Far too many well-meaning grandparents put themselves into serious financial distress by paying for their child's attorney fees, moving expenses, and car loans. It is important that you avoid making this mistake.

If you decide to lend your child money, do it in a formal way. Write down the terms of the loan. Include a repayment schedule and a reasonable rate of interest. If your child is likely to receive a financial settlement as part the separation or divorce, arrange to have the loan repaid in full on the settlement date.

Be especially cautious about lending large amounts of money for things such as legal fees. Custody battles can eat up thousands and thousands of dollars. If you decide to help with legal fees, expect to be asked more than once. Family law cases tend to move along slowly and often take unexpected (and costly) twists and turns. Think carefully about whether or not your contribution will help move things in a peaceful direction or simply add fuel to a wildfire. Not having the money to fight in court can motivate parents to explore other options.

7. *Pour love into your grandkids*: Children of separation and divorce often struggle with feeling invisible. While their parents fight over them, it is common for the kids to begin feeling lonely, rejected, alienated, and angry. While maintaining a neutral posture, do your best to remind the children that they are loved, that the custody dispute will eventually come to an end, and that it is up to their parents to work things out. Avoid making derogatory remarks about either of their parents.

   Go to recitals, baseball games, and karate class. Send them a card or take them for an ice cream. Invite them to the movies. Let them teach you how to play Nintendo or ride a skateboard. If they start getting into trouble at school, or in the community, teach them some healthy ways to work out their problems.

   Be available to your grandkids if they want to confide in you. Be a good listener. If they request information about the specifics of their parent's dispute, ask them to talk with their parents about that. If you would like to get a book on this subject for your grandchild, *Mom's House Dad's House for Kids*, would be an excellent choice. World renowned author and family expert, Isolina Ricci, teaches kids how to survive the emotional ups and downs of a custody dispute in this easy-to-read book for kids, ages nine and up.

8. *If they move in:* Should you decide to let your child and grandchildren move in with you, make sure you set out ground rules in advance. The kinds of issues that need to be thought through include:
   - Who is going to pay for food and utilities
   - How long will they be staying
   - Will you be expected to provide day care? If so, when and for how long?

- Who will transport the kids to school and activities?
- What about chores?
- Will you be expected to discipline the kids? If so, how?

9. *If your case involves domestic violence, child abuse, or substance abuse:* If domestic violence, child abuse, or serious substance abuse has been alleged (or are present) in your child's custody dispute, you may be asked by the court to supervise your child's visits with your grandchildren. Before agreeing to do this, make sure that you fully understand what will be expected of you in terms of reporting to the court on what occurs during the visits you supervise. This is a big responsibility that could entangle you in the custody mess and potentially jeopardize your relationship with one or both parents. One alternative you might consider is recommending that the parents use a professional visitation monitor. A professional monitor will supervise visits in a park, at a restaurant, in a private home, or at their office. They will then submit a written report to the court. A list of court recognized visitation monitors will be available at your local courthouse or online.

10. *Take good care of yourself:* A custody dispute is exhausting on everyone involved. Make sure to take good care of yourself. Go to church, get some extra exercise, eat healthy food, and make sure you get to bed at a reasonable hour. If you sense you are getting overwhelmed, talk with an old friend, a pastor, or a counselor. Resist the temptation to become too invested in how the custody dispute turns out. If you stay focused on remaining neutral, take care of your self, and pour love into your grandchildren, everything else should work out on its own.

The International Center for Peaceful Shared Custody

All over the world, parents are struggling with the confusion, frustration, anger, grief, expense, isolation, and fear that fighting over sharing custody can provoke. It doesn't need to be this way. The tools to prevent this are available. Educating parents about their options is the key.

The International Center for Peaceful Shared Custody is a first-of-its-kind non-profit (501c3), parent-driven, online community that connects families struggling with separation or divorce with the tools, strategies, professionals, and programs being used by families who are thriving in spite of their breakup.

Online at PeacefulSharedCustody.com, the Center provides a range of free and unique tools for parents, grandparents, step-parents, and anyone else involved in a shared-custody dispute. Here's what you'll find:

- **Shared Custody First-Aid**: A triage station designed to welcome and direct battle-weary parents toward resources that can help them improve their situations right away
- **Peace Builder's Community**: Have you ever wanted to ask other divorced or separated parents for advice on how to handle a shared-custody problem? The Peace Builder's Community allows you to tap into a global community of parents, and do just that.
- *What Works* **Directory**: The internet's largest compilation of material related to divorce and separation, including research papers, books, videos, trainings, success stories, and more.
- *A New Way to Win* **Trainings**: A broad selection of live and on-demand trainings on shared-custody topics chosen by parents, grandparents, stepparents, and others.

- **Find Professionals and Programs**: Connect with local ADR-focused professionals and programs committed to promoting peaceful shared custody.

Join our global community and help families by lending your voice, experience, energy, and creativity to the cause of promoting peaceful shared custody.

Additional Resources Available Online

The following can be downloaded free of charge at www.
ANewWaytoWin.com:

Finding the Right Professionals
- Top Ten Questions to Ask a Family Law Attorney
- What is Collaborative Divorce?
- Top Ten Questions to Ask a Collaborative Divorce Lawyer
- What is Private Mediation?
- Top Ten Questions to Ask a Private Mediator
- What is a Shared-Custody Coach?
- Top 10 Questions to Ask a Shared-Custody Coach
- What is Parent Coordination?
- Top Ten Questions to Ask a Parent Coordinator
- Top Ten Questions to Ask a Mental Health Professional
- Essential Questions to Ask your Doctor Before Putting Your Child on Mental Health Medicines

For Grandparents
Helping Our Adult Children: A Framework for Grandparents

Problem Solving
Five Simple Steps for Resolving Shared-Custody Problems

The Language of De-escalation
The Principles of Shared Custody Verbal Aikido

Bibliography

Association of Family and Conciliation Courts (AFCC). (2005) *Guidelines for Parent Coordination.* Family Court Review, 44, 164-181.

Association of Family and Conciliation Courts (AFCC). (2006) *Planning for Shared Parenting: A Guide for Parents Living Apart.*

Barlow, D., & Craske, M. (2007). *Mastery of your Anxiety and Panic.* New York: Oxford Press

Blakeslee, S., Lewis, J., & Wallerstein, J. (2000). *The Unexpected Legacy of Divorce.* New York: Hyperion.

Byrne, R. (2006). *The Secret.* New York: Atria Books.

Chopra, D. (2000) *Perfect Health: The Complete Mind/Body Guide.* New York: Three Rivers Press.

Eddy, B. (2006). *High Conflict People in Legal Disputes.* Scottsdale: HCI Press.

Emery, R. (2004). *The Truth about Children and Divorce: Dealing with the Emotions So You and Your Children can Thrive.* New York: Penguin.

Fisher, R. & Shapiro, D. (2006). *Beyond Reason: Using Emotions as You Negotiate.* New York: Penguin/Viking.

Fisher, R., & Ury, W. (1981). *Getting to Yes: Negotiating Agreement Without Giving In.* Boston: Houghton Mifflin Company.

Garrity, C.B., & Baris, M.A. (1994). *Caught in the Middle: Protecting the Children of High-Conflict Divorce.* New York: Lexington Books.

Goldstein, A., & McGinnis, E. (1997). *Skillstreaming the Elementary School Child: New Strategies and Perspectives for Teaching Prosocial Skills.* Champaign, IL: Research Press.

Glasser, W. (1998). *Choice Theory: A New Psychology of Personal Freedom.* New York: Harper Collins Publishers.

Hartson, J., & Payne, B. (2006) *Creating Effective Parenting Plans: A Developmental Approach for Lawyers and Divorce Professionals.* Chicago: American Bar Association.

Johnston, J., Kuehnle, K., & Roseby, V. (2009) *In the Name of the Child: A Developmental Approach to Understanding and Helping Children of Conflicted and Violent Divorce.* New York: Springer Publishing.

Kabat-Zinn, J. (1990) *Full Catastrophe Living: Using the Wisdom of Your Body and Mind to Face Stress, Pain and Illness.* New York: Dell Publishing

Kabat-Zinn, J. (1994). *Wherever you Go, There You Are: Mindfulness Meditation in Everyday Life.* New York: Hyperion.

Kubler-Ross, E. (2005). *On Grief and Grieving: Finding the Meaning of Grief Through the Five Stages of Loss.* New York: Scribner.

Lyster, M. (2007). *Building a Parenting Agreement That Works: How to Put Your Kids First When Your Marriage Doesn't Last.* Berkeley: Nolo Press.

Lyubomirsky, S. (2007). *The How of Happiness: A New Approach to Getting the Life You Want.* New York: Penguin Group.

Mosten, F. (2009). *Collaborative Divorce Handbook: Helping Families without Going to Court.* San Francisco: Jossey-Bass.

Pullen, J. R. (1998). *The Life Skills Program.* San Diego, CA: Life Skills and CHAANGE Anxiety Treatment Programs.

Rawls, J. (2001). *A Theory of Justice.* Cambridge: Belknap Press of Harvard University Press.

Ricci, I. (1997). *Mom's House Dad's House: Making Two Homes for Your Child.* New York: Fireside.

Ricci, I. (2006). *Mom's House Dad's House for Kids: Feeling at Home in One or Two.* New York: Fireside.

Roberts, E. (2006). *Should You Medicate Your Child's Mind?: A Child Psychiatrist Makes Sense of Whether to Give Kids Psychiatric Medication.* New York: Marlowe & Company.

Seligman, M. (2007). *The Optimistic Child: A Proven Program to Safeguard Children Against Depression and Build Lifelong Resilience.* New York: Houghton Mifflin Books.

Stewart, R. (2001). *The Early Identification and Streaming of Cases of High-Conflict Separation and Divorce.* Justice Department of Canada.

Ury, W. (2007). *The Power of a Positive No: Save The Deal, Save The Relationship—and Still Say No.* New York: Bantam Dell.

Weil, A. (2007). *8 Weeks to Optimum Health: A Proven Program for Taking Full Advantage of Your Body's Natural Healing Power.* New York: Ballantine Books.

About the Author

Tobias Desjardins, LCSW, is a private child-custody mediator, and a licensed therapist specialized in working with separation and divorce. Mr. Desjardins is the Founder and Executive Director of the International Center for Peaceful Shared Custody, a non-profit organization that connects families struggling with separation or divorce with the tools, strategies, professionals, and programs being used by families who are thriving in spite of their breakup.

Mr. Desjardins is also the Director of Prevention Network, a provider of court-ordered shared-custody education programs in Los Angeles, Riverside, San Bernardino and San Diego counties.

Before moving to California in 2000, Mr. Desjardins was the Executive Director of Trillium Family Resources—a Canadian non-profit organization based in Montreal, Canada.

From 2000–2005, Mr. Desjardins was a member of a Riverside County Department of Mental Health crisis psychiatric team, where he worked primarily with families of divorce or separation where a child was at risk of committing suicide.

Mr. Desjardins lives in Southern California with his wife and three children.

Training

A New Way to Win **- Training Series**
A FREE series of conference call trainings hosted by Tobias Desjardins and featuring internationally acclaimed guests.

Video Blog
Once a week, experts from the family law field will answer your shared-custody questions.

Attend a Court-Approved Workshop with the Author
Tobias Desjardins offers a one-day Co-parenting Workshop in Los Angeles. Always scheduled on a Saturday (8:30am –5:30pm), the workshops offer parents, step-parents, and grandparents the opportunity to work directly with the author in a small group setting. The workshop focuses on the following:
- The stages of divorce or separation
- How to build a successful co-parenting plan
- Effectively managing co-parenting conflict
- How to discuss sensitive topics with your children
- Negotiating with a difficult Ex
- Understanding step-family dynamics
- Avoiding the most common co-parenting mistakes

Participants receive a certificate at the end of the day. This workshop is on the list of Family Law Court approved programs in Los Angeles, Riverside, San Bernardino and San Diego counties. For more information please go to www.WhatIsCoparenting.com

CPSIA information can be obtained at www.ICGtesting.com
Printed in the USA
LVOW091028180112

264416LV00003B/218/P